The Legal Rights of Union Stewards

ROBERT M. SCHWARTZ

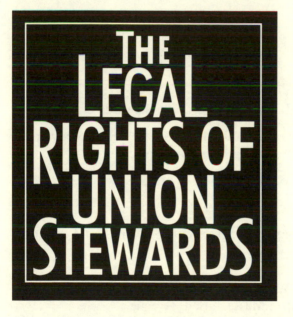

THE LEGAL RIGHTS OF UNION STEWARDS

ILLUSTRATIONS BY NICK THORKELSON

Second Edition

work rights press

BOSTON, MASSACHUSETTS

The Legal Rights of Union Stewards

Copyright © 1988, 1994 by Robert M. Schwartz
Ninth printing 1998, with revisions

Printed in the United States of America

ISBN 0-945902-01-8

Library of Congress Catalog Number: 94-060761

Work Rights Press
678 Massachusetts Avenue
Box 391887
Cambridge, MA 02139
Telephone: 1-800-576-4552

Also available from Work Rights Press are *The Legal Rights of Union Stewards* (Spanish edition) and *The FMLA Handbook: A Practical Guide to the Family and Medical Leave Act for Union Members and Stewards*, by Robert M. Schwartz (1996). See last page for ordering information.

GCIU

To my wife,
Emily Sedgwick,
Shop steward (1985-1987)
ACTWU Local 377 (New Bedford, MA)

Table of Contents

Detailed Table of Contents

Chapter 4: Union Right to Information   53

Chapter 5: "Weingarten Rights"

PREFACE

THIS handbook explains the rights of union stewards and suggests ways to enforce them. It draws on my experience practicing union-side labor law and conducting training programs at union conferences, meetings, and workshops.

The book is designed to supplement the steward manuals prepared by various unions. Its goals are to encourage stewards to feel more secure about their status and to provide legal tools to help stewards do their jobs.

Admittedly, using labor law to fight management is a two-edged sword. Delays, technicalities, and political influences can subvert legal processes. Unions sometimes place too much reliance on the law when they would have better success taking group action.

Nevertheless, unions are stronger when they demand that their legal rights be respected. This does not always require formal charges. Insisting on a legal right to a supervisor, plant manager, or labor relations official can sometimes win compliance. Raising the likelihood of National Labor Relations Board (NLRB) charges can also be effective. If you do file formal charges, consider additional measures, such as rallies, petitions, work-to-rule campaigns, and picketing. The best strategy *combines* direct action with legal action to exert maximum pressure on an employer.

Before taking action based on this book, please heed the following cautions:

Don't jump to conclusions. The materials, questions, and answers in this handbook are based on National Labor Relations Board (NLRB) decisions. You may be tempted to assume that an answer applies to you because your situation is similar to that described in the question. This can be dangerous. Just one slight difference in your workplace can alter the application of a legal rule. Moreover, labor law rules are not permanent. The NLRB may change settled policies. In the 1980s, for example, many union rights were weakened as a result of decisions by NLRB members appointed by President Ronald Reagan. President Bill Clinton's appointees, who took office in 1994, in part reversed course. If at all possible, consult a labor attorney or knowledgeable union official before filing charges.

Make sure you are covered. This handbook relies on decisions which apply the National Labor Relations Act (NLRA). The NLRA applies to most employees in the private sector. It does not cover *state and local government employees*. Many states, however, have public-sector labor laws similar to the NLRA (except for the right to strike), and state labor boards often look to NLRA decisions for guidance. Check with your state labor board to verify your rights and complaint procedures.

Also excluded from the NLRA are *federal, railroad, and airline employees.* These employees are covered by labor laws which differ from the NLRA in many respects. *Farm workers* are also omitted from the NLRA.

Don't expect the law to answer all of your questions. The NLRA regulates four areas of labor relations: organizing, bargaining, contract administration, and strikes. Although each of these subjects is important to stewards, this handbook concentrates on contract administration, especially grievance handling. Even within this area, many issues are not covered by the NLRA or any other law. For example, the NLRA does not answer questions such as, "What is the time limit for filing a grievance?" or, "Can stewards use work time to investigate grievances?" Answers to these and other questions not covered by the labor laws depend on contract language, workplace rules, and past practices.

Don't take unnecessary risks. Even when a legal right clearly applies to something you are doing, or want to do, it is important to act with care — especially if you are considering refusing or disregarding a management order or rule. If you are fired, it may take months and sometimes years to get your job back through legal measures. Don't put your job on the line unless your union and fellow workers have the strength to prevent management from taking reprisals against you.

Footnotes. The footnotes provide additional information as well as references to NLRB decisions. Stewards and unions can cite or submit these labor cases to arbitrators and NLRB investigators. If you want to read the entire case, try to locate a library that subscribes to the NLRB services. Likely depositories include federal and state courthouse libraries, law school libraries, and large public or university libraries. Your international union headquarters may have a library that will send you cases. Work Rights Press will also send you copies of NLRB cases. See page 181 for ordering information.

Acknowledgements (second edition). I was helped in this edition by several friends in the labor movement, including Phil Mamber, Steve Early, and James Duarte. Muriel Randolph and Louise Greenleaf did an excellent job preparing the manuscript and Nick Thorkelson, as usual, contributed a top-notch design.

I value readers' comments, suggestions, and criticisms. You may write to me at 20 Winthrop Square, Boston, MA 02110, or call me at (617) 695-1976. When using this book, please remember the maxim: "If you don't know, learn. If you do know, teach."

Robert M. Schwartz

INTRODUCTION

*The Union Steward**

ho are these of lowly pay
With haggard look and hair of grey?
They get no rest by day or night.
They're always wrong. They're never right.
They do not have a law degree,
But go to bat for you and me.
Though seldom have they been to college,
They must possess the widest knowledge,
Of labor grades and when to grieve,
Vacation pay and sickness leave.
Of overtime and who's to do it,
Of coffeetime and who's to brew it.
The how and which and why and when,
And all the problems of women and men.
If, with forepersons they agree,
Then they're rats who've got weak knees.
If, to the workers they try to cater,
They're branded as agitators.

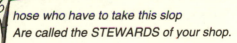

*hose who have to take this slop
Are called the STEWARDS of your shop.*

— Anonymous

* With apologies to the anonymous poet, the steward's gender has
been broadened.

ARE YOU a steward, committeeperson, delegate or other union grievance representative?

If so, you are part of an extraordinary group, estimated to number more than 250,000 men and women, in 53,000 local unions across the United States. Union stewards represent departments, shifts, and work-sites. They monitor collective-bargaining agreements, advise employees on contract provisions, confront employers over safety issues, and represent employees in grievance proceedings.

A steward's job is important and exciting. You protect the jobs and welfare of your fellow employees and use your leadership skills to build the union.

Your position, however, is not without perils. To be effective, you must protest management actions that violate the collective-bargaining agreement, are arbitrary or unfair, or threaten the health or safety of employees. In response, management may try to intimidate or harass you or impose discipline.

To prevent reprisals — and to gain management's respect — you must be well prepared. Your most valuable tools are union solidarity, contract rights, and labor law rights.

Union solidarity. This is the militancy and determination of the employees you represent. A steward backed by a unified group, willing to act if the steward is attacked, has significant freedom of action.

Contract rights. A strong union contract forbids discrimination against union activities, guarantees time for union business, and provides superseniority for union representatives.

Labor law rights. Federal and state labor laws prohibit interference with legitimate union activities, protect stewards in presenting grievances, force employers to supply grievance information, and require employers to bargain before making changes that affect employees.

CHAPTER 1
The National Labor Relations Act

THE MOST important law for U.S. workers is the National Labor Relations Act.[1]

The NLRA was enacted by Congress in 1935. It was hailed at the time and for many years after as the Magna Carta of American labor. Previously, employers had been free to spy on, interrogate, discipline, discharge, and blacklist union members. But in the 1930s workers began to organize militantly. A great strike wave in 1933 and 1934 included citywide general strikes and factory takeovers. Violent confrontations occurred between workers trying to form unions and the police and private security forces defending the interests of anti-union employers. Some historians believe that Congress adopted the NLRA primarily in the hopes of averting greater, possibly revolutionary, labor unrest.

The NLRA guaranteed workers the right to join unions without fear of management reprisal. It created the National Labor Relations Board (NLRB) to enforce this right and prohibited employers from committing unfair labor practices that might discourage organizing or prevent workers from negotiating a union contract.

The NLRA's passage galvanized union organizing. Successful campaigns soon followed in the automobile, steel, electrical, manufacturing, and rubber industries. By 1945, union membership reached 35% of the workforce. In reaction, industrialists, and other opponents of organized labor sought to weaken the NLRA. They succeeded in 1947 with the passage of the Taft-Hartley Act, which added provisions to the NLRA allowing unions to be prosecuted, enjoined, and sued for a variety of activities, including mass picketing and secondary boycotts.

The last major revision of the NLRA occurred in 1959, when Congress imposed further restrictions on unions in the Landrum-Griffin Act.

Key Provisions

The most important sections of the NLRA are Sections 7, 8, and 9.

Section 7 is the heart of the NLRA. It defines *protected activity*. Stripped to its essentials, it reads:

> Employees shall have the right to self-organization, to form, join, or assist labor organizations, to bargain collectively through representatives of their own choosing, and to engage in other concerted activities for the purpose of collective bargaining or other mutual aid and protection.

Section 7 applies to a wide range of union and collective activities. In addition to organizing, it protects employees who take part in grievances, on-the-job protests, picketing, and strikes.

Section 8 defines employer *unfair labor practices.* Five types of conduct are made illegal:

- Employer interference, restraint, or coercion directed against union or collective activity (Section 8(a)(1))
- Employer domination of unions (Section 8(a)(2))
- Employer discrimination against employees who take part in union or collective activities (Section 8(a)(3))
- Employer retaliation for filing unfair-labor-practice

charges or cooperating with the NLRB (Section 8(a)(4))

• Employer refusal to bargain in good faith with union representatives (Section 8(a)(5))

Threats, warnings, and orders to refrain from protected activities are forms of interference and coercion that violate Section 8(a)(1). Disciplinary actions, such as suspensions, discharges, transfers, and demotions, violate Section 8(a)(3). Failures to supply information, unilateral changes, refusals to hold grievance meetings, and direct dealings violate Section 8(a)(5).

Section 8 also prohibits union unfair labor practices, which include, according to legal construction, failure to provide fair representation to all members of the bargaining unit.[2]

Section 9 provides that unions, if certified or recognized, are the exclusive representatives of bargaining-unit members. It prohibits the adjustment of employee grievances unless a union representative is given an opportunity to be present, and establishes procedures to vote on union representation.

The NLRA sets out general rights and obligations. Enforcing the Act in particular situations is the job of the NLRB.

The National Labor Relations Board (NLRB)

The NLRB is a federal agency with headquarters in Washington, D.C. It has 33 regional offices throughout the country. (See Appendix for addresses.)

Election petitions and unfair-labor-practice charges are filed at the regional office level. NLRB regional directors issue unfair-labor-practice complaints and make decisions in election disputes. Administrative law judges (ALJs) conduct hearings on unfair-labor-practice complaints.

The NLRB is headed by a five-person panel called the Board. Board members are appointed by the President, after approval by the Senate, for staggered five-year terms. The Board hears appeals from decisions of regional directors and ALJs. Board decisions in unfair-labor-practice cases can be appealed to the federal circuit courts and the U. S. Supreme Court.

Unfair-Labor-Practice Charges

When an employer violates the NLRA, a union, a steward, or an employee can file an unfair-labor-practice charge at the NLRB regional office that covers the place of employment. Charges may be filed in person or by mail. Call the NLRB for charge forms. Punishment of, or threats against, employees who file NLRB charges is strictly forbidden. *Charges must be filed at the NLRB, and served on the employer, within six months of the violation.*

After receiving the charge, the NLRB regional director appoints a Board agent to investigate. The agent interviews the union and the employer, obtains signed statements (affidavits), and explores the possibility of settlement. Usually within 30 days, the agent makes recommendations to the regional director, or his or her representative, who determines whether to:

1. issue a formal complaint against the employer;
2. dismiss the charge; or
3. defer the charge.

If the Board investigation reveals that the charge has merit, the Board agent will usually encourage the employer to settle the case and comply with the Act. If the employer agrees, the agent will prepare a written agreement in which the employer agrees to post a notice to employees of the settlement terms.

Note: Sometimes the Board agent will suggest to the union that it accept an employer's "non-Board" settlement of the case and withdraw its charge without a posting. Unions that want a stronger result should refuse to withdraw and insist that the agent obtain a written Board agreement with a posting.

Formal complaints. An NLRB complaint describes the alleged violation and sets a date and place for a hearing before an ALJ. Hearings are usually held within three to nine months. At the hearing, an NLRB attorney presents the case against the employer. The union may take part.

After the hearing, the ALJ issues a decision and a *recommended order*. If the union prevails, the order will usually require the employer to cease its illegal actions, comply with the Act, and post a notice for 60 days informing employees of the terms of the order. When employees have been suspended or discharged, the ALJ can recommend reinstatement with seniority, back pay, and interest. The ALJ cannot impose fines or punish supervisors.

If neither side appeals, the ALJ's order is adopted by the Board and becomes final and binding. If the employer or the union appeals, the case is reviewed by the Board in Washington. The Board can affirm, modify, or reverse the ALJ's decision.

The de minimis policy. Regional directors sometimes decline to issue complaints because the employer's violation is considered isolated, insignificant, or, to use a Latin phrase, "de minimis."[3] For example, a supervisor may make a veiled threat to a steward. But if the supervisor apologizes, and the threat is not repeated, the regional director may dismiss the charge on de minimis grounds.

Deferral. In a case called *Collyer Insulated Wire Co.* (1971), the NLRB adopted a *deferral policy* towards certain unfair-labor-practice charges.[4] Under the policy, regional directors are required to defer (hold-off) issuance of a complaint if the union has filed, or can file, a contract grievance against the employer's alleged wrongdoing and if arbitration is available under the contract. The NLRB then waits to see whether the grievance resolves the matter. If the grievance is settled or arbitrated, the regional director reviews the results. Usually, the director defers to the grievance settlement or the arbitration decision and dismisses the union's charge (or asks the union to withdraw). But if the director determines that the settlement or arbitration decision is "clearly repugnant to the Act" and "palpably wrong," he or she can issue a complaint and set the case down for an NLRB hearing.[5]

The NLRB justifies its deferral policy as a way of conserving the agency's resources when alternate means to resolve a dispute are available. Unions oppose defer-

ral because it diminishes their statutory right to have unfair-labor-practice violations decided — without union expenses — by the NLRB.

At one stage in the years after *Collyer*, the NLRB did not defer charges alleging discrimination against union representatives.[6] In 1984, however, President Reagan-appointed Board members expanded the deferral policy to include these violations.[7] Now, even discharges of union officers are deferred. On the other hand, charges alleging refusals to provide information,[8] or retaliation for filing charges at the NLRB,[9] are usually not deferred. Deferral is also denied if the employer raises procedural barriers, such as that the time limit for filing a grievance has expired.[10]

If the NLRB is likely to defer, why file unfair-labor-practice charges? Even when deferral is probable, there are reasons to file unfair-labor-practice charges:

1. The NLRB will conduct at least a preliminary investigation of the charge. In the course of the investigation, the employer may become educated about union NLRA rights and agree to settle the matter.

2. If the NLRB defers, and the case goes to arbitration, the union can show the arbitrator the NLRB deferral letter, remind the arbitrator that his or her decision will be reviewed by the regional director, and encourage the arbitrator to apply NLRA principles in deciding the grievance.[11]

3. If the arbitrator makes a decision that contradicts NLRA principles, the NLRB may issue a complaint and provide relief to the union. In many cases, the NLRB has reinstated stewards despite an arbitrator's award sustaining discharge.[12]

QUESTIONS AND ANSWERS

1. Filing a charge

Q. Does the union need a lawyer to file an NLRB charge?

A. No. You can get blank copies of the charge form from the NLRB regional office. The form does not have to be typed. You can mail it in (with four copies). You can also go to the regional office to obtain assistance in filling it out. The regional office will serve the charge on the employer (although you should do this yourself if you are near the end of the six-month limitations period). See page 19 for a sample charge.

2. Subsection numbers

Q. Most of the NLRB charge form is easy to fill out but one question is confusing. In blank 1h., we are supposed to designate the subsections of Section 8 that are being violated. What should we do if we are not sure of the correct subsection numbers?

A. Leaving out the subsection numbers will not hurt you. The Board agent will help you correct any mistakes by amending the form later. You could also write "all sections" in the space provided.

Note: All employer violations of the Act are violations of Section 8(a)(1) — whether or not they also violate one of the other sections.

3. Description of violation

Q. How detailed should we be in describing the violation on the NLRB charge form?

A. Not very! You will have a full opportunity to explain your case to the Board agent. On the charge form simply state the bare bones of what happened. One or two sentences should be sufficient. Do not name your witnesses.

Note: You may allege more than one violation on the same form. Number each allegation.

4. Are affidavits confidential?

Q. If I sign an affidavit for a Board agent investigating an unfair-labor-practice charge, will my employer be given a copy?

A. Not during the investigation stage. But if the case goes to complaint, a hearing is held, and you testify, your affidavit will be supplied to counsel for the employer prior to your cross examination.[13] Otherwise, employers may not question you about what you told the NLRB or ask you for a copy of your affidavit. Retaliation against you because you provide information to the NLRB, or testify against your employer at a hearing, is illegal.

5. Appealing a dismissal

Q. If the regional director dismisses the union's unfair-labor-practice charge, can the union appeal?

A. Yes. You have 14 days to appeal by letter to the NLRB General Counsel in Washington, D.C. The General Counsel can instruct the regional director to issue a complaint. But if the General Counsel sustains the regional director's decision to dismiss the charge (as usually happens), there is no further appeal to the Board or the courts.

6. Preliminary injunction

Q. If a steward is fired for illegal reasons, can the NLRB apply for a court order to put the steward back on the job pending resolution of the case?

A. Yes, but the union will have to work hard to get this to happen. After issuing a complaint, the regional director has authority, when circumstances are compelling, to request a preliminary injunction from a federal court to restore the status quo.[14] Unions should request injunctive relief in writing on the charge form or by letter to the regional director.

7. Legal expenses

Q. If the union hires a lawyer to file an unfair-labor-practice charge at the NLRB, and the Board rules in the union's favor, will the employer be ordered to pay for the union's legal expenses?

A. No — except in an extreme case where the Board determines that the unfair labor practice was flagrant and the employer's defense was frivolous.[15]

8. Delays

Q. If an employer appeals an ALJ decision, how long could it take to get the decision enforced?

A. By appealing an ALJ's decision to the Board, and then appealing the Board's decision to the courts, an employer can delay compliance for two or more years.

9. Arbitrator's award insufficient

Q. A steward in our bargaining unit was discharged for remarks she made during a grievance session. The union filed a charge at the NLRB but the regional director sent us a letter deferring the case to the grievance process. The union took the case to arbitration and the arbitrator reinstated the steward. But the arbitrator said that the steward's conduct was not 100% proper and denied any back pay. Should the union ask the NLRB to reopen this case?

A. Yes. If the steward's conduct comes under Section 7 of the Act, the regional director can issue a complaint seeking full back pay for the steward.[16]

10. Statute of limitations

Q. Does the NLRB ever allow charges to be filed more than six months after a violation?

A. Only rarely. The six-month limitations rule is strictly enforced. An exception occurs, however, if the union, for legitimate reasons, was unaware of the violation or if the employer concealed its illegal actions from the union. In such cases, the six-month period begins when the union becomes aware of the violation.[17]

11. Retaliation

Q. If the NLRB dismisses my unfair-labor-practice charge, can I be disciplined by my employer?

A. No. It is unlawful to retaliate against an employee for filing at the NLRB — even if the NLRB dismisses the charge.

12. Airline workers

Q. We work for American Airlines. Does this book apply to us?

A. No. Airline workers are not covered by the NLRA. The airline and railway industries are regulated by the Railway Labor Act (RLA).[18] The RLA does not allow unions or employees to file unfair-labor-practice charges.

13. School teachers

Q. How much of this book applies to school teachers?

A. Possibly, quite a bit. State and local government employees are not covered by the NLRA. However, many states have public-sector collective-bargaining laws modeled after the NLRA. Public-sector bargaining laws are enforced by state labor boards. The major distinction between public- and private-sector labor laws is that public-sector employees, with few exceptions, are prohibited from striking.

14. Construction stewards

Q. Does this book apply to stewards in the construction industry?

A. Yes and no. The construction industry comes under the jurisdiction of the NLRA and the labor law rules in this book are applicable. However, in many of the building trades, full-time business agents handle representational duties, including monitoring the collective-bargaining agreement and presenting grievances.

15. Federal employees

Q. Are federal employees covered by the NLRA?

A. No. Federal employees come under the jurisdiction of the Civil Service Reform Act of 1978, which established the Federal Labor Relations Authority (FLRA).[19] The FLRA follows many, but not all, of the rules described in this book. Federal employees may not strike.

16. Postal workers

Q. I work for the U.S. Postal Service. Am I covered by the NLRA?

A. Yes. In 1970, Congress placed the Postal Service under the jurisdiction of the NLRA. Postal workers can file unfair-labor-practice charges at the NLRB but do not have the right to strike.

CHAPTER 2
The Special Status of Union Stewards

B Y ITS VERY nature, a union steward's job involves confrontation. On the shop floor, in supervisors' offices, and in grievance meetings, stewards must defend the actions of employees and contest those of management. Often this can be done in a calm and straightforward manner, i.e., "quiet diplomacy." But you may sometimes feel compelled to raise your voice, argue forcefully, threaten job protests, or emphasize the union's position in other vigorous ways.

Vigorous advocacy, however, conflicts with the usual rules of employee conduct, which stress obedience to, and respect for, supervisors and managers. If stewards had to abide by these rules, they would face an impossible dilemma: either hold back when defending employees or risk almost certain discipline.

In recognition of their dual capacities, the NLRB has adopted special rules for stewards and union officers.

The Equality Rule

Under NLRB doctrine, stewards and union officers have a protected legal status. When engaged in representational activities, stewards and union officers are considered to be *equals* with management. Behavior which could otherwise result in discipline must be tolerated. The NLRB describes the equality rule this way:

The relationship at a grievance meeting is not a "master-servant" relationship but a relationship between company advocates on one side and union advocates on the other side, engaged as *equal opposing parties* in litigation.[20]

The equality rule is consistent with declarations of the U.S. Supreme Court, which has said that the NLRA protects "robust debate" and "gives a union license to use intemperate, abusive, or insulting language without fear of restraint or penalty if it believes such rhetoric to be an effective means to make its point."[21]

The equality rule allows a steward to raise a voice, gesture, use "salty" language, challenge management's claims of truthfulness, threaten legal action, or raise the possibility of group protests. Vigorous advocacy may not always be appropriate or necessary, but when it is used, an employer cannot label it as insubordination and impose discipline.

When does the equality rule apply? The equality rule applies when a steward acts in his or her *representational* capacity. It does not apply when a steward acts in his or her *individual* capacity.

You are acting in your representational capacity when you investigate a grievance, request information, present a grievance, or otherwise represent employees.

You are acting in your individual capacity when you discuss your own work assignments, work performance, or compliance with work rules. Being a steward does not mean you have a license to tell management off at all times and places.

Limits. The equality rule does not provide 100% equality. Employers may discipline stewards for representational conduct which (in the NLRB's words) is "outrageous" or "indefensible" and is "of such serious character as to render the employee unfit for further service."[22] A steward may not use extreme profanity, racial epithets, or threats of violence, and may not, under any circumstances, strike a supervisor. Nor do stewards enjoy legal protection if they organize slowdowns or work disruptions, lead contract-barred work stoppages, or file grievances in bad faith.

Note: The line between protected and unprotected conduct is not precise — and supervisors often exaggerate when describing a steward's behavior. To protect yourself, bring an employee or fellow union representative to grievance sessions or other meetings with management.

The No-Reprisal Rule

The right to engage in concerted activities, protected by Section 7 of the NLRA, includes

participation in grievance activities. A steward cannot be punished or threatened with punishment because management considers his or her grievances to be overly frequent,[23] petty,[24] or offensively written.[25] Nor may management threaten a steward with adverse consequences if the steward brings a grievance to a higher step.

Reprisals against stewards are unfair labor practices. An employer violates the no-reprisal rule if it:

- Orders a steward to perform more difficult or unpleasant work[26]
- Gives a steward an unfavorable evaluation[27]
- Denies a steward pay opportunities[28]
- Segregates a steward from other employees[29]
- Deprives a steward of overtime or other benefits[30]
- Enforces plant rules more strictly against a steward[31]
- Threatens a steward with physical harm or strikes a steward[32]
- Overly supervises a steward[33]
- Transfers a steward to a different job or shift[34]
- Gives a steward a poor reference for a prospective job[35]

The Same-Standards Rule

Some supervisors take the attitude that stewards can be held to higher standards than other employees. "Of all people, you're supposed to know the rules," is often heard when a steward is given a penalty for coming in late or making a production error. Other supervisors take the position that stewards are supposed to set examples for other employees.

These attitudes have no support in logic or in law. Stewards are not super-workers. Who would take the post if it meant higher work requirements or more severe discipline?

Under NLRB rules, employers must apply the same standards to stewards as they do to other employees. Employers violate the same-standards rule if they hold stewards to higher standards or impose more severe discipline for similar misconduct.[36]

The only circumstance in which a steward may be held to a higher standard than a rank-and-file employee occurs when a no-strike clause in a union contract imposes affirmative duties on union officials. For example, if a no-strike clause says that the union will "exert itself to bring about a quick termination of such violation," an employer may discipline union officers and stewards more severely than rank-and-filers for taking part in a mid-contract walkout.[37]

Note: Even if a no-strike clause does not impose affirmative duties, a steward may be disciplined for instigating or leading a contract-barred work stoppage or slowdown.[38]

NLRB Charges

In most cases involving discrimination against stewards, the union will be able to file a contract grievance as well as an NLRB charge. The union should file with the NLRB at the same time that it files its grievance. See below for a sample charge.

As discussed in Chapter 1, the NLRB usually defers discrimination charges, including discharge cases, to the

Sample NLRB Charge

FORM NLRB-501 (11-88)	UNITED STATES OF AMERICA NATIONAL LABOR RELATIONS BOARD CHARGE AGAINST EMPLOYER	FORM EXEMPT UNDER 44 U.S.C. 3512	
		DO NOT WRITE IN THIS SPACE	
		Case	Date Filed

INSTRUCTIONS:
File an original and 4 copies of this charge with NLRB Regional Director for the region in which the alleged unfair labor practice occurred or is occurring.

1. EMPLOYER AGAINST WHOM CHARGE IS BROUGHT

a. Name of Employer	b. Number of workers employed
Keystone Press	Approx. 100

c. Address (street, city, state, ZIP code)	d. Employer Representative	e. Telephone No.
100 Myrtle Street Chicago, IL 60634	Morris Palmer, Pres.	965-1972

f. Type of Establishment (factory, mine, wholesaler, etc.)	g. Identify principal product or service
Press	Books

h. The above-named employer has engaged in and is engaging in unfair labor practices within the meaning of section 8(a), subsections (1) and (list subsections) _____ of the National Labor Relations Act, and these unfair labor practices are unfair practices affecting commerce within the meaning of the Act.

2. Basis of the Charge (set forth a clear and concise statement of the facts constituting the alleged unfair labor practices)

On July 23, 1994, the employer threatened to retaliate against Steward Charles Murray because of Mr. Murray's representation of a bargaining unit employee.

By the above and other acts, the above-named employer has interfered with, restrained, and coerced employees in the exercise of the rights guaranteed in Section 7 of the Act

3. Full name of party filing charge (if labor organization, give full name, including local name and number)
Printing Workers Local 100

4a. Address (street and number, city, state, and ZIP code)	4b. Telephone No.
100 Baker Street Chicago, IL 60641	965-9622

5. Full name of national or international labor organization of which it is an affiliate or constituent unit (to be filled in when charge is filed by a labor organization)

International Printing Workers Union AFL-CIO

6. DECLARATION

I declare that I have read the above charge and that the statements are true to the best of my knowledge and belief.

By *Leonard Bralowitz*	President, Local 100	
(signature of representative or person making charge)	(title if any)	8/1/94
Address 20 Union Street, Chicago, IL 60603	965-4770	
	(Telephone No.)	(date)

WILLFUL FALSE STATEMENTS ON THIS CHARGE CAN BE PUNISHED BY FINE AND IMPRISONMENT (U. S. CODE, TITLE 18, SECTION 1001)

contractual grievance procedure. Nevertheless, filing an
NLRB charge strengthens the union's position. Charges
alleging employer threats may escape deferral, especially if the collective-bargaining agreement limits the
authority of an arbitrator to issue a cease-and-desist
order.[39]

QUESTIONS AND ANSWERS

1. Shaking a finger

Q. During a grievance session, I shook my finger at the
plant manager. He said, "If you ever do that again,
you're finished here." Could he really fire me for this?

A. No. Shaking a finger falls well below the level of
"outrageous" conduct forbidden of stewards.[40] File an
NLRB charge because of the threat.

2. Shouting

Q. After a grievance meeting with management, I
received a written warning for "extremely loud behavior." Aren't I allowed to raise my voice?

A. Yes. If it does not disturb production, loud arguing
during a grievance meeting, or even shouting, is protected
by the NLRA.[41]

3. Calling supervisor a liar

Q. At a grievance session, I called my supervisor a liar.
As it turned out, I was mistaken. Can I be disciplined?

A. No. Under the equality rule, a steward has a protected right to accuse a supervisor of lying — even if the
accusation turns out to be incorrect.[42]

4. Calling boss a jackass

Q. During a grievance meeting, my foreman made a number of ridiculous statements. Infuriated, I called him a "jackass." Can I be disciplined?

A. Not legally. "Salty" language during grievance meetings, short of extreme profanity, is protected by the NLRA. In one case, the NLRB allowed a steward to call a supervisor "a big twerp."[43] In another, the NLRB reinstated a steward who called his boss "a stupid ass."[44] In a third case, the NLRB removed the written reprimand of a

steward who told his supervisor, "I don't give a f__k who you call."[45]

5. Continuing to argue

Q. I had a heated grievance argument with my supervisor. After ten minutes, he declared, "This meeting is over, go back to work." I continued to argue for a couple of minutes. Can I be disciplined for not immediately obeying his order?

A. Not legally. The NLRB says that a short *cooling-off* period must be tolerated after the end of a grievance discussion as "it is unrealistic to believe that the principals involved in a heated exchange can check their emotions at the drop of a hat."[46] Protection may be lost, however, if a steward refuses *repeated* back-to-work orders.[47]

6. Slamming door

Q. I got angry during a meeting with the plant manager, walked out, and slammed the door. Can I be disciplined?

A. Not legally. Tempers often flare during grievance meetings. Slamming a supervisor's door is not so outrageous as to warrant a denial of Section 7's special protections for union representatives.[48]

7. Going too far

Q. During a conversation with her supervisor, a steward lost her temper, screamed, told him he should have his mouth bashed in, and said that she was going to do it. Several employees stopped work to listen. Then she dared the manager to fire her — which he did. The steward has apologized, but the company has refused to reinstate her. Do we have a good case at the NLRB?

A. Probably not. There are limits to a steward's actions. In this case, the steward threatened physical violence. Moreover, her outburst took place near other employees and disrupted work.[49]

Note: Even when a steward's conduct goes over the line, it may receive NLRA protection under the theory of *provocation* — if the employer's outrageous actions or denial of union rights provoked the steward's reaction.[50]

8. Telling steward to "shut up"

Q. Can a supervisor tell a steward to "shut up" during a grievance meeting?

A. This depends. If the full sentence is, "Shut up and listen to what I am saying," it is legal, as part of the give-and-take allowed in grievance meetings. But if the supervisor says, "If you don't shut up, you'll be out the door," the supervisor has made an illegal threat.[51]

9. Suing steward for slander

Q. At a grievance meeting, I claimed that a supervisor had altered an employee's time records. The supervisor said she was going to sue me for slander. Can she win?

A. No. Statements during grievance or arbitration sessions are *legally privileged*, which means they cannot serve as the basis of a slander lawsuit.[52]

Note: The immunity against slander or libel suits does not apply outside the grievance-arbitration process. For example, unions and union officials can be sued for knowingly publishing false statements about supervisors in leaflets or union newspapers.[53]

10. Personal criticism

Q. My boss attacked me, calling my grievances "nit-picking" and a "waste of time." Is this allowed?

A. Yes. The NLRA permits employers to criticize unions and union representatives.[54] Only comments which reach the level of harassment, or contain threats, are illegal.

11. Warning for encouraging grievances

Q. I have been encouraging employees to file grievances against supervisors who do bargaining-unit work. Yesterday, a supervisor told me, "If I find out that you're soliciting grievances against me, it'll mean your job." Is this an NLRA violation?

A. Yes. Encouraging employees to file grievances is protected union activity.[55]

12. Loss of promotion

Q. My supervisor is upset because of the number of grievances I file. Last week, he suggested I slow down if I hope for a promotion. Is this an unfair labor practice?

A. Yes. The supervisor is threatening you for filing grievances.[56]

13. Warning for poor work

Q. Two days after I filed a set of grievances, I was given a warning for "substandard work." The charge is bogus. Should I file at the NLRB?

A. Yes. If the warning is because of your union activities, it is unlawful. The timing of the reprimand suggests retaliation. Evidence that management was upset with the grievances will strengthen your case.[57]

14. Over-supervising steward

Q. Ever since I was elected steward, management has been watching me. Sometimes when I work, three bosses stare at me for hours. Is this legal?

A. No. Supervising stewards more closely than other workers is a form of coercion which violates the NLRA.[58] Line up your witnesses. Then file an NLRB charge.

15. Imposing new standard

Q. Before I became a steward, my supervisor never said anything about my work performance. Now I get a warning every time I make a mistake. Is this an NLRA violation?

A. Yes. It is union discrimination when an employer tolerates an employee's deficiencies for years, and then changes its attitude because the employee becomes a steward.[59]

16. Veiled threat

Q. When I presented a grievance, my boss told me, "If you don't like it around here, you can always quit." NLRA violation?

A. Yes. This is a *veiled threat*. Your boss is warning you that your union activity is incompatible with your job.[60]

17. Enforcing plant rule more strictly

Q. A plant rule requires employees to remain in their work areas during work time. The rule is never enforced — except for me. Is this an NLRA violation?

A. Yes. Enforcing plant rules more strictly against stewards violates Section 8(a)(3).[61]

18. Setting example

Q. The day before Christmas, a few employees, including myself, celebrated at work with a few beers. A supervisor reported us. The other workers received warnings, but I was hit with a suspension. The boss said, "You're the union steward and are supposed to set an example." Can he do this?

A. Not legally. It violates the NLRA to hold a steward to a higher standard of conduct than other employees or to impose unequal punishment.[62]

19. Failure to follow grievance procedure

Q. I received a disciplinary warning because I filed a written grievance before presenting it orally as specified in the first step in our grievance procedure. Can the company get away with this?

A. Not legally. A technical mistake by a steward in grievance processing, even one that violates the contract, cannot be used as a basis for discipline. Your employer may be able to reject the grievance, or can protest to the union, but it violates the NLRA if it takes action against you.[63]

20. Threatening steward to obtain information

Q. In preparing for a promotion grievance, I compiled quite a bit of documentation. The company has asked for my records and threatened to suspend me if I refuse to comply. Can it do this?

A. No. Although the union may have an obligation to supply the information requested (see Chapter 4, Question 30), an employer may enforce this obligation only by filing an NLRB unfair-labor-practice charge *against the union*. Threats directed at individual union representatives are unlawful.[64]

21. Questioning employees about steward's actions

Q. The company thinks I am organizing a slowdown. Can supervisors question employees about what I have told them to do?

A. Only to a limited extent. Interrogation of employees about union activity is a sensitive legal area. The following rules apply:
1. Employees must be told the reason for the questions.
2. Employees must be told that the interviews are voluntary and that they may decline to take part.
3. Employees must be told that no reprisals will be imposed because of what they say or do not say.
4. The interviews must not be coercive in nature.[65]

22. Telling employees not to answer questions

Q. The company is interviewing employees about drug use in the plant. If I tell my people not to answer questions, could I get into trouble?

A. Yes. Union representatives may not obstruct a legitimate investigation of misconduct.[66] If management learns of such orders, you could be disciplined.

23. Advising employee to refuse a work order

Q. An employee was instructed to work overtime on a job which he is not qualified to perform under the contract. Can I advise the employee to refuse the job?

A. Not safely. One of the most hallowed rules in labor relations is, "obey now — grieve later." This rule applies even when the employer's order plainly violates the contract. A steward may be disciplined for encouraging insubordination.[67]

The U.S. Supreme Court has said that actions taken to implement a collective-bargaining agreement are protected by the NLRA unless conducted in an "abusive" manner or if they violate a contract's no-strike clause.[68] However, the NLRB sometimes takes the position that open insubordination removes an employee from Section 7's protections.[69]

Note: The chief exception to the "obey now — grieve later" rule concerns unsafe work. Arbitrators generally allow employees to refuse work assignments which involve unusually dangerous safety or health hazards that are normally not part of the job.[70]

24. Refusal to relay supervisor's instructions

Q. Three employees were told by their supervisor to go to a motivational seminar after work. They were reluctant

to go so the supervisor asked me to tell them to attend the program. Could I be punished if I refuse to do so?

A. Not legally. Stewards do not have to relay supervisors' orders. The responsibility to direct employees lies solely with management.[71]

25. Speaking up during meetings

Q. Our manager likes to call department meetings to lecture us. When she asks for responses, can I criticize management?

A. Yes. Union representatives have a right to speak up at employee meetings as long as the employer has not forbidden employee comments.[72]

26. Advising employee not to sign warning slip

Q. Can I advise an employee not to sign a warning slip if the warning is out of line?

A. Not necessarily. If a company rule requires employees to sign warning slips, you risk an insubordination charge if you advise an employee to refuse to sign. Although the NLRB has sometimes aided stewards in this kind of situation,[73] the most prudent course is to have the employee write "signed under protest" before his or her signature.

27. Wildcat strike

Q. Workers in my department walked out over a speed-up. I did not call the walkout but I did participate. Since we have a no-strike clause in our contract, we were punished. Most employees received three-day suspensions, but I was given six days because I am the steward. Isn't this illegal discrimination?

A. Not necessarily. The lawfulness of your discipline depends on the no-strike clause. If the clause obligates the union to take active steps to prevent work stoppages, or bring them to an end, union representatives have special responsibilities and the employer may impose greater punishment against stewards.[74]

28. Suing steward for work stoppage

Q. Can a steward be sued for money damages for taking part in a contract-barred work stoppage?

A. No. Neither union representatives nor rank-and-file employees can be held personally liable for money damages for taking part in strikes — even when the strike violates the contract.[75] (The employer may, however, be able to sue the union.)[76]

29. Strike to reinstate steward

Q. A steward was fired because she used a swear word during a grievance session. This leaves the third shift without union representation. If the union calls a walk-out, will we have any legal protection? (We are subject to a no-strike clause.)

A. Possibly — but there is definite risk. According to Supreme Court and NLRB decisions, employees can strike despite a no-strike clause if the employer commits a *serious NLRB violation* which undermines the union.[77]

Note: A union must have strong organizational support before conducting a mid-contract walkout. Otherwise, the employer is likely to sue the union for lost profits and expenses.

30. Filing court complaint against supervisor

Q. My supervisor took a swing at me during a griev-ance session. Can I file an assault-and-battery complaint against him?

A. Yes. Section 7 protects a steward who files a crimi-nal complaint against a supervisor who uses violence against legitimate union activities.[78]

Note: Stewards are also legally protected when filing complaints with state or federal labor or anti-discrimina-tion agencies on behalf of bargaining-unit employees.[79]

31. Steward pin

Q. Our union gave us steward pins. Can I get into trou-ble for wearing mine to work?

A. Ordinarily, no. Employees have a protected right to wear steward pins and other union insignia at work.[80] An exception may apply, however, if "special circum-stances" exist such as an employer's established busi-ness plan, consistently enforced by pre-existing appearance rules, to present a particular public image. But even when employees wear uniforms and have contact with the public, the NLRB has sanctioned the wearing of small nonprovocative union pins.[81]

32. Constructive discharge

Q. Since I became a union committeeman, I have been subjected to harassment from management including threats, reduction in my hours, and even a demotion in rank. I know I can file grievances and NLRB charges, but I am so demoralized I feel I have to quit now. Could I do this and also file at the NLRB?

A. Yes. When an employee resigns because of intolerable working conditions, it is termed a "constructive discharge." If the NLRB concludes that the cause of your resignation was the employer's unlawful harassment, it can order the harassment stopped and reinstate you with full back pay.[82]

CHAPTER 3
The Grievance Process

LMOST all collective-bargaining agreements contain a grievance and arbitration procedure to resolve contract violations and other employee and union disputes. There is a wide spectrum of procedures. In some unions, such as those in the building trades, business agents handle disputes. In most unions, however, stewards investigate, file, and present grievances. There are usually three or four "steps" (meetings) involving progressively higher-level union and management personnel. The last step is usually a hearing before a professional arbitrator whose decision on the grievance is final and binding. Employers violate the NLRA if they interfere with the grievance process, adjust grievances without the union, or unreasonably delay grievance meetings.[83]

Filing Grievances

Employees for whom a grievance is filed are called "grievants." They are protected by Section 7 of the NLRA. Grievants may not be retaliated against, threatened, or harassed because of their good-faith grievance activity. Management commits an unfair labor practice if it:
- Uses harsh language to intimidate a grievant[84]
- Increases a penalty because a grievance is filed[85]
- Lays off an employee for pursuing a grievance[86]

- Threatens an employee for testifying at a grievance hearing or arbitration[87]

Soliciting Grievances

There is a widespread notion (undoubtedly employer-encouraged) that stewards may not "solicit" grievances. According to the notion, stewards may not seek out contract violations and must wait until employees bring them complaints. This notion is false. According to the NLRB, "The solicitation of grievances is a protected activity for stewards as well as other employees."[88] Stewards can encourage employees to file grievances. Indeed, stewards can even post notices or distribute literature urging employees to file.

Note: Collective-bargaining agreements sometimes say that grievances must be signed by the affected employee. Nevertheless, legal decisions have ruled that unions can sign grievances as the employee's agent.[89] The NLRA protects a steward who signs an employee's name to a grievance with no intent to deceive the employer.[90]

Investigating Grievances

Unless specified otherwise in a collective-bargaining agreement, stewards can interview employees and investigate grievances before and after work and during breaks.

To the surprise of some, however, nothing in the NLRA guarantees stewards the right to conduct union business during work hours. Employers may enforce rules or contract provisions restricting grievance investigations during such hours.[91]

Many union contracts permit stewards a "reasonable" amount of time, or a specified number of hours, during work to conduct union business. Other unions have this right by virtue of consistent past practice. In such work-places, any unilateral attempt by management to reduce union-business time is an unfair labor practice (as well as a contract violation).[92]

Adjusting Grievances

One of the least understood parts of the NLRA is Section 9(a). This section is important enough to be quoted in full:

> Representatives designated or selected for the purpos-es of collective bargaining by the majority of the employ-ees in a unit appropriate for such purposes, shall be the exclusive representatives of all the employees in such unit for the purposes of collective bargaining in respect to rates of pay, wages, hours of employment, or other condi-tions of employment: *Provided,* That any individual employee or a group of employees shall have the right at any time to present grievances to their employer and to have such grievances adjusted, without the intervention of the bargaining representative, as long as the adjustment is not inconsistent with the terms of a collective-bargain-ing contract or agreement then in effect: *Provided further,* That the bargaining representative has been given oppor-tunity to be present at such adjustment.

Section 9(a) recognizes the union as the exclusive representative of bargaining-unit employees. No indi-vidual employee or group of employees is allowed to bargain with the employer over terms and conditions of employment.

The first proviso in Section 9(a) permits individual employees or groups of employees to *present* "grievances" (which the NLRB defines as contract grievances or other complaints)[93] without going through the union. This allows management to have a private conversation with an employee who has a complaint or wants a change in his or her job assignment, pay, hours, or other working conditions.

The second proviso in Section 9(a) protects the union. It forbids employers from "adjusting" (settling) an employee's grievance unless the union is given an opportunity to be present. An employee can complain about his or her work or request changes, but a supervisor *cannot agree to a change* without calling in a union representative. For example, an employee can complain about his or her vacation schedule, but management cannot change the schedule unless the union is notified. The union must be notified even if the employee is against the union's presence.[94] The union's job is to make sure the adjustment is consistent with the collective-bargaining agreement and is fair to other employees.

Adjusting a grievance privately with an employee is called "direct dealing." It is a Section 8(a)(5) unfair labor practice. A charge may be filed at the NLRB.

Denying a grievance is a form of adjustment. An employer commits an unfair labor practice if it refuses an employee's grievance without first calling in a union representative.[95] A violation also occurs if the employer makes an offer to the employee, whether or not agreement is reached.[96]

Note: A union can give up ("waive") its Section 9(a) rights by agreeing to contract language that permits supervisors to adjust grievances with employees alone.[97] This language is sometimes found in the clause setting out the first step of the grievance procedure. If contract language is ambiguous, past practice determines whether the union has waived its Section 9(a) right to be present at grievance adjustments.

Sample Description of Violation for NLRB Charge Form ("Basis of Charge")

> On September 14, 1994, the employer adjusted an employee's grievance by changing the employee's hours without notifying the union and allowing it to be present.

Supporting Grievances

Filing a grievance does not eliminate the union's right to use collective action. To the contrary, many unions organize support for grievances. Although strikes and walkouts may be barred by a no-strike clause, several tactics may be utilized. These include:

- Distributing leaflets about the grievance during breaks or before or after work[98]
- Sending a letter to the head of the parent corporation[99]
- Circulating a petition in support of the grievance[100]
- Holding a meeting of employees during a break or at mealtime to discuss the grievance[101]
- Leading a delegation of employees to the labor relations office during a break carrying signs supporting the grievance[102]
- Writing letters to local newspapers about the grievance[103]

- Picketing the home of the manager or supervisor responsible for deciding the grievance (in an orderly and non-violent manner)[104]
- Establishing informational picket lines at the work-place (picketing which publicizes the grievance but does not interfere with employees, suppliers, or shippers) unless the contract bars picketing[105]
- Wearing tee-shirts or pins with slogans supporting the grievance[106]

The above activities, if sponsored by the union, or consistent with the union's position, are protected by Section 7 of the NLRA. Workers who take part cannot be threatened or punished.

QUESTIONS AND ANSWERS

1. Intimidating grievant

Q. After an employee filed a grievance, her supervisor approached her and angrily said, "Hey stupid, what's the big idea of calling in the union?" Is this allowed?

A. No. Employers violate the NLRA if they make intimidating statements to discourage employees from filing grievances.[107] File an NLRB charge.

2. Transferring grievant

Q. One day after a truck driver filed a grievance, he was transferred from his regular route without any reason given. Is this illegal?

A. Possibly. If the employer is retaliating against the employee because of his grievance, it violates the NLRA.[108]

3. Increasing discipline because grievance is filed

Q. Our supervisor told me she plans to suspend a worker for loafing. When I said the union would grieve it, she replied, "In that case, I'm going to fire him." If she does, do I have an NLRB case?

A. Yes. Increasing a penalty because a grievance is filed, or because of an intention to file one, is unlawful.[109]

4. Discouraging use of the grievance process

Q. After she filed a grievance, an employee's supervisor suggested that she would do better to speak directly to the plant manager about the problem without the union. Is this legal?

A. No. Telling an employee that she has a better chance of resolving a grievance without the union discourages use of the grievance process and interferes with the employee's right to be represented. This violates the NLRA.[110]

5. Threat to reduce work

Q. We filed a grievance challenging the way the company computes Sunday pay. The company says that if the union's position turns out to be correct, it will have to discontinue Sunday work. Isn't this an illegal threat?

A. Not necessarily. An employer may make a good-faith prediction, if based on legitimate facts.[111]

6. Are contract violations unfair labor practices?

Q. Last week, the company clearly violated the seniority rights of an employee. We filed a grievance. Should we also file an unfair-labor-practice charge at the NLRB?

A. Probably not. The NLRB does not consider contract violations, even obvious ones, to be sufficient evidence of bad faith to constitute an unfair labor practice.[112]

Note: An exception to this rule applies if the violation is a significant mid-term *modification of the contract*, such as a failure to make payments to union benefit funds or to remit union dues.[113]

7. Filing grievances after contract expires

Q. Our collective-bargaining agreement has expired. Negotiations are at an impasse. If we choose to work without a contract, can we still use the grievance procedure to contest disciplinary actions?

A. Yes. As a general rule, contractual terms and conditions, if not part of a bargaining impasse, must be continued after contract expiration. An employer may not terminate the grievance procedure unless this was one of the demands made by management prior to reaching impasse.[114]

Note: An exception to the above rule applies to the obligation to arbitrate. Generally, employers may refuse to arbitrate grievances based on events occurring after the contract's expiration date.[115]

8. Employer criticizes grievance

Q. Can a supervisor tell employees that the union is "crazy" to file a grievance and that the union leadership "doesn't know how to read a contract" ?

A. Yes. The NLRA allows employers to criticize union actions so long as there is no threat of retaliation.[116]

9. Employer survey of union support

Q. We filed a grievance disputing the qualifications of several employees who are working overtime in the mixing department. The company foreman has been asking employees in the mixing department if they support the grievance. Is this legal?

A. No. This is a form of direct dealing. An employer may not question employees to survey the degree of union support.[117] File an NLRB charge.

10. Attempt to bribe steward

Q. We have a militant steward whom the company is attempting to bribe by offering a management job. Could we file an NLRB charge?

A. Yes — but it may be difficult to prove the case. Offering a management position to a union steward violates the NLRA if the union can prove that the purpose of the offer is to induce the steward to stop filing grievances or to take less militant positions.[118]

11. Confidentiality between steward and employee

Q. An employee was discharged for fighting. As his steward, I interviewed him Can the company require me to disclose my interview notes?

A. No. The relationship between a steward and a worker subject to discipline is *confidential.* An employer may not question a steward about a conversation that the steward has with such an employee. According to the NLRB, such a conversation "constitutes protected activity in one of its purest forms."[119]

12. Employer interrogations — prior to disciplinary action

Q. The company is interviewing employees as part of an investigation into on-site gambling. Can management require employees to answer questions?

A. Yes. Unions and employees do not have a legal right to obstruct a legitimate investigation of employee misconduct. Prior to disciplinary action being taken, employees may be required to answer investigatory questions.[120]

Note: Employees should always request a union steward before answering questions relating to misconduct. The steward may be able to suggest ways to avoid bringing harm to themselves or fellow union members (see Chapter 5).

13. Employer interrogations — after disciplinary action

Q. Arbitration is scheduled on a discharge case. Can the employer compel union witnesses to submit to interviews prior to the arbitration date?

A. No. An employer cannot compel employees to submit to interrogations on a matter after discipline has been imposed on the matter and the union has grieved. Employees who refuse to submit to questioning in order to support fellow employees are protected by Section 7 of the NLRA.[121]

Note: Employers are also restricted when questioning employees to prepare for an unfair-labor-practice proceeding. Here, the NLRB insists that the employer: (1) inform the employee of the true reasons for the interview; (2) notify the employee that the interview is voluntary and the employee can decline to take part; and (3) assure the employee that no reprisals will be taken because of what the employee might say or not say.[122]

14. Interference with union rights

Q. Our contract permits stewards four hours per week time off to investigate grievances. Yesterday I needed a pass to investigate a grievance for a part-time employee. My supervisor said that the part-timer is not covered by the contract (untrue) so I should return to my job. Is this an NLRA violation?

A. Yes. Although you always take a risk by disobeying a direct order from management, it is important to insist that your rights to investigate grievances be respected.

The NLRB has ruled that a steward can refuse an order from a supervisor who is attempting to prevent the steward from engaging in legitimate union business, if the union business is allowed by the contract or past practice, does not disrupt the work of other employees, and does not constitute an attempt to avoid work.[123]

Arbitrators have also recognized an exception to the traditional "obey now — grieve later" rule when management gives an order that conflicts with established union rights.[124]

15. Discipline for spending too much time on union business

Q. Our contract permits stewards to spend "a reasonable amount" of work time in the performance of union business. Yesterday, after spending 10 minutes investigating a grievance, I was given a disciplinary warning for "spending too much time away from work." Can I file an NLRB charge?

A. Yes. According to the NLRB, a steward has certain rights when a collective-bargaining agreement or past practice allows stewards time off for union business but does not cap the amount. The employer may not discipline a steward for excessive time off without *first* notifying the union of the problem and attempting to come to an *accommodation*. The two sides must attempt to balance the steward's right to time off with the employer's right to productive work.[125]

16. Fining informer — in the absence of a pending grievance

Q. A union member told management that warehouse workers were sleeping on the job. The union fined the member for informing on others. Is this legal?

A. Yes. In the absence of a pending grievance, a union can take action against a member who informs on fellow members[126] — unless the employee is a group leader, foreman, or supervisor who is required to report misconduct.[127]

17. Fining informer — after grievance filed

Q. Several employees were discharged for taking part in a sick-out. Prior to the grievance hearing, a union member gave damaging information to management. Can we expel or fine her for harming fellow union members?

A. No. A union cannot punish a member for giving information to management after discipline has been imposed and a grievance has been filed. This is considered improper interference with the grievance process.[128]

Note: It is also an NLRA violation to discipline a member for *testifying* for the employer at a grievance or arbitration hearing.[129] This rule also applies to management. Employers may not punish supervisors whose testimony during grievance or arbitration hearings aids the union's case.[130]

18. Tearing up grievance

Q. I presented a grievance to my supervisor. He said it was worthless and tore it up in front of me and two other employees. Should I file an NLRB charge?

A. Yes. Destroying grievance papers in an abusive manner violates the duty to bargain in good faith.[131]

19. Disregard for union

Q. Our employer, a nursing home, has no respect for the union. The human relations manager cancels grievance meetings, makes us wait weeks to meet again, walks out when meetings get started, and keeps us waiting for long periods for what is inevitably a rejection. What can we do?

A. The most effective way to overcome disrespect is through *organization*. Mobilizing the membership to confront management — through petitions, rallies, non-cooperation campaigns, and the like — should get results. You could also file an unfair-labor-practice charge at the NLRB. A pattern of refusing to meet or bargain over grievances violates the NLRA.[132]

20. Putting grievance settlement in writing

Q. We are settling a subcontracting grievance. If we request that the settlement be put in writing and signed, does management have to comply?

A. Probably, yes. Although there is apparently no Board decision directly on the issue, Section 8(d) of the NLRA, which defines collective-bargaining obligations, requires the parties to sign "a written contract incorporating any agreement reached if requested by either party." Grievance meetings are integral parts of the collective-bargaining process.[133]

21. Refusal to discuss grievances with particular steward

Q. Can the company refuse to meet with a steward on the grounds that the steward "lies all the time?"

A. No. Unions pick their representatives, not management. Union choices must be respected. In the absence of violent or abusive behavior by a steward, an employer violates the NLRA by refusing to meet.[134]

22. Tape recording grievance meeting

Q. At a first-step grievance meeting, management insisted on tape recording the proceedings despite union objections. Did the company violate the NLRA?

A. Yes. If grievance meetings have traditionally not been recorded, it is unlawful to unilaterally institute taping procedures.[135] File a charge at the NLRB (see Chapter 6 on unilateral changes).

23. Impact on others

Q. I am handling a grievance for an employee who walked off the job without permission. I would like to remind management that another employee did the same thing two years ago without punishment. Could I get this employee in trouble by mentioning his name?

A. The NLRB has two rules on this question. The first rule states that an employer cannot take action against an employee whose *misconduct was known* to management prior to the employee being identified by the union in a grievance proceeding.[136] Otherwise, the employer could, in effect, punish the union for pursuing a grievance.

The NLRB's second rule says that if the union reveals *misconduct that was totally unknown* to management, the employer can act on this information and impose discipline.[137] In your case, if management, or at least some level of supervision, was aware of the other employee's walk-out two years ago, the union can freely cite this occurrence as an example of unequal discipline.

24. Accommodations for disabled employee

Q. An employee suffered a serious back injury in an automobile accident. She called the company to request a return to work on a light-duty job. Can management accede to her request without bringing in the union?

A. Not necessarily. It is certainly arguable that the employee's request comes under Section 9(a) of the NLRA which requires that a union be notified and have input before an employer resolves an employee's grievance.[138] However, the NLRB has not yet ruled on whether light-work requests trigger Section 9(a) obligations.

25. Employer contacts grievant

Q. A worker was fired. The union filed a grievance but the company contacted the worker and offered her a cash settlement. Is this allowed?

A. No. This is direct dealing. The company has committed an unfair labor practice — even if the employee rejects the company's offer.[139]

26. Employer pressure to drop grievance

Q. We are in negotiations on a new collective-bargaining agreement. The employer is insisting that the union withdraw a pending grievance. It won't move on the contract unless we agree. Is this legal?

A. No. An employer can *ask* a union to withdraw a grievance, but it commits an unfair labor practice if it *insists* on withdrawal as a condition to a new contract.[140]

27. Employee involvement committee

Q. Our company has set up an "employee involvement committee" to meet with managers on a regular basis to come up with suggestions to improve the "quality of work." It seems to us that the company is trying to skirt the union. Are these programs legal?

A. Not always. Section 8(a)(2) of the NLRA bans employer-created or employer-dominated labor organizations. Labor organizations are defined as groups or committees which: (1) include employees; and (2) "deal" with management on issues relating to wages, hours, or working conditions. If the employee involvement committee is purely a discussion group, it may be legal. But if the committee comes up with proposals for changes, and management responds to these proposals, the union can file an unfair-labor-practice charge seeking its dissolution.[141]

28. Refusal to arbitrate

Q. The company is refusing to arbitrate because it says the grievance has nothing to do with the contract. We disagree. Is there any way to get the grievance to arbitration?

A. Yes. Depending on the arbitration service designated in your contract, you may be able to process the case even though your employer contests "arbitrability." The American Arbitration Association, for example, schedules hearings even if the employer refuses to cooperate.[142] Alternatively, the union can file a lawsuit to compel the employer to submit to arbitration.[143] Filing an NLRB charge will probably not help because the NLRB usually takes the position that a refusal to arbitrate a single grievance is not sufficient to constitute an unfair labor practice.[144]

29. Appealing arbitration decision

Q. If we lose an arbitration case, can we appeal to the courts?

A. Yes, but it probably won't get you anywhere. The courts offer a very narrow opening for the review of labor arbitrations. Judges usually deny appeals if there is a "plausible basis" for the arbitration decision.[145] Only if the decision is completely at variance with the contract,[146] or if the arbitrator failed to be impartial during the hearing, is a court appeal likely to succeed.

30. Wearing button to support grievance

Q. I am a chief steward. In support of a subcontracting grievance, I had a button made saying, "Bargaining, Not Blackmail!" The company said it will not conduct further grievance discussions with me if I wear the button. Do I have any rights?

A. Yes. NLRB case law recognizes the right of union representatives to wear buttons to grievance meetings.[147] The company must meet with you despite the button.

31. Letters to customers

Q. To support a grievance against unsafe working conditions, can the union write letters to customers to explain the situation and ask for support for our stand?

A. Yes. Letters to customers are protected by the NLRA as long as the letters are truthful and do not attack the quality of the employer's products or services.[148]

32. Leaflets

Q. In my off-duty hours, can I put leaflets about a grievance on car windshields in the employee parking lot?

A. Usually, yes. Unless the contract forbids leafleting, an off-duty employee has a Section 7 right to distribute literature to employees in non-working areas.[149] According to the Board, "except where justified by business reasons, a rule which denies off-duty employees entry to parking lots, gates, and other outside nonworking areas will be found invalid."[150]

33. Overtime-refusal campaign

Q. To support a grievance against subcontracting, does the union have legal protection in calling on employees to refuse overtime assignments?

A. Not necessarily. The legal status of overtime refusal campaigns depends on whether overtime is mandatory or voluntary. If the collective-bargaining agreement says that employees must work requested overtime, or if the contract is silent but employees have always worked requested overtime, a campaign to refuse overtime assignments would not be protected.[151] But, if the contract states that overtime is voluntary, or if employees have the right to refuse overtime by virtue of consistent past practice, an overtime-refusal campaign would be protected by Section 7 of the NLRA.[152]

CHAPTER 4

Union Right to Information

ONE OF the most useful tools provided by the NLRA is the union's right to obtain information from employers. Although this right is not explicit in the text of the Act, the U.S. Supreme Court and the NLRB have construed it from Section 8(d) which requires employers and unions to "bargain collectively." Without access to information, unions cannot effectively fulfill their responsibilities to negotiate, monitor, and enforce contracts. Refusals to provide information, or unreasonable delays, are unfair labor practices in violation of Section 8(a)(5) of the Act.

Note: The NLRB does *not* defer unfair-labor-practice charges which allege a refusal to provide information.[153] Unions win a majority of these cases. Aggressive use of NLRB charges to enforce union information rights is highly recommended. See page 61 for a sample charge.

When To Request Information

Employers sometimes assert that union information rights are restricted to data needed for contract negotiations. This is not true. In *NLRB v. Acme Industrial Company (1967)*, the Supreme Court ruled that employers must furnish unions with information relevant to contract enforcement.[154]

As a steward, you may request information:
- To monitor compliance with the contract
- To investigate whether a grievance exists
- To prepare for a grievance meeting
- To decide whether to drop a grievance or move it up the ladder
- To prepare for an arbitration hearing

What You Can Request

The employer obligation to provide grievance information is extremely broad. It includes the disclosure of documents, factual information, and data.
Management must provide
requested materi-
als

that
could be
useful to the
union or could
lead to the identification of
useful information. If the
employer does not have the information
in its possession, it must make a diligent effort to obtain it,

including making requests of third parties with whom it has a relationship (such as contractors, customers, and parent corporations).[155]

Union requests must be made in good faith. The union must have a genuine suspicion, based on employee complaints or other evidence, that the contract has been violated. It cannot use the information duty to harass the employer or to conduct a "fishing expedition" into the employer's records.

Information requests are good tactics for unions. They help to win grievances and make employers think twice about violating the contract. *Information requests should be submitted for almost all grievances.*

Documents. You are entitled to examine a wide variety of employer documents prior to filing or arguing a grievance. Here are some of the records you can request:

- accident reports
- attendance records
- bargaining notes
- bonus records
- collective-bargaining agreements for other bargaining units or other facilities
- company manuals and guidelines
- company memos
- contracts with customers, suppliers, and subcontractors
- correspondence
- customer complaints
- customer lists
- disciplinary records
- equipment specifications
- evaluations
- inspection records
- insurance policies
- interview notes
- investigative reports
- job assignment records
- job descriptions
- material safety data sheets (MSDS's)
- payroll records
- personnel files

- photographs
- piece-rate records
- reports and studies
- security guard records
- security reports
- seniority lists
- supervisors' notes
- time study records
- training manuals
- videotapes
- wage and salary records
- work rules

Factual information. Employers must answer pertinent factual questions. For example, in a discharge case, you can ask for all reasons for the discharge and the names and addresses of witnesses who supplied information on which the discharge decision was based. In a subcontracting grievance, you can ask for the name and address of the contractor, the date of the contract, a description of the work, the amount of the contract, the reasons for the subcontract, and prior occasions on which work has been subcontracted.

Data. Employers must provide you with lists, statistics, and data.. For example, you can request lists of prior discipline for particular infractions, statistics on pension contributions, or the amounts of bonus payments to employees. When is comes to data, employers are not excused from compliance because of the size of the union's request (although the company may insist on cost reimbursement).[156] Information requests going back as long as five years have been enforced by the NLRB.[157]

General inquiries. Unions may make general informational requests such as:

- "Please supply all documents or records which refer to or reflect the factors causing you to reject this grievance."
- "Please supply all factual bases for the company's decision."
- "Please provide all documents relied upon by the company in the discipline of the employee."

Disciplinary grievance. When grieving a warning, suspension, or discharge, *always* request a copy of the grievant's personnel file. Also, since "unequal punishment" is often the best theory to win a case, ask for information about other employees who have committed the same offense. In some cases, you can request information about supervisors and non-bargaining-unit employees (see this chapter, questions 12 and 13).

Contract interpretation grievance. If the grievance requires interpretation of contract language, request the employer's notes from the bargaining sessions that negotiated the disputed clause; the dates and contents of any union statements upon which the employer is relying; and the dates and descriptions of any practices or events which the employer contends support its position.

Promotion grievance. Request the personnel file of the successful bidder, as well as the file of the grievant. Request copies of interview notes and documents evaluating the applicants.

Past-practice grievance. If you are trying to enforce a past practice, and management contends that the practice is inconsistent, request dates and descriptions of all occasions when management claims a departure from the practice.

Health-and-safety grievance. If you are grieving an unsafe substance, request a list of workers made sick by the substance, the material safety data sheet (MSDS) supplied by the manufacturer, copies of OSHA citations, and any studies by the employer concerning the substance. When necessary, the union may arrange for an outside specialist, such as an industrial hygienist, to conduct an inspection of the workplace.[158]

Sample Requests

Although an information request may be made orally, it is best to put it in writing, date it, and *keep a copy*. Be as specific as possible in identifying the information you are seeking. Here are two examples of information-request letters:

To: Paul O'Connor, Labor Relations Manager
From: Anne Thompson, Steward
Re: Discharge of James Hamilton for tardiness
Date: June 10, 1994

Dear Mr. O'Connor:

In order to prepare the grievance of James Hamilton, I am requesting the following information from the company:

1. James Hamilton's personnel file.

2. The tardiness records of all bargaining-unit employees over the past three years.

3. The names of all employees disciplined for tardiness within the past three years, dates and descriptions of each discipline, and the amount of tardiness that led to each discipline.

This request is made without prejudice to the union's right to file subsequent requests. Please provide the information by June 24, 1994. If any part of this letter is denied or if any material is unavailable, please provide the remaining items as soon as possible, which the union will accept without prejudice to its position that it is entitled to all documents and information called for in the request.

Sincerely,

Anne Thompson

To: Charles Brooks
From: Paul Hillier
Re: Subcontracting grievance (painting work)
Date: October 10, 1994

Dear Mr. Brooks:

The union hereby requests the following information to prepare for the processing of the union's grievance.

1. Please list each occasion on which the company sub-contracted painting work from July 1, 1993 to the present.

2. For each project subcontracted, please state the reasons why the company did not assign the work to bargaining-unit personnel.

3. Please state the names of each contractor hired by the company to do painting work since July 1, 1993.

4. Please provide copies of all correspondence between the company and said contractors.

5. Please provide copies of all contracts between the company and said contractors.

6. Please state the amount of money paid to said contractor for each project and attach invoices from said contractors.

7. Please state the wage rates paid to employees of said contractors on all painting projects.

This request is made without prejudice to the union's right to file subsequent requests. Please provide the information by October 24, 1994. If any part of this letter is denied or if any material is unavailable, please provide the remaining items as soon as possible, which the union will accept without prejudice to its position that it is entitled to all documents and information called for in the request.

Sincerely,

Paul Hillier
President, Local 520

Note: Unions can prepare master information-request forms and distribute them to stewards.

Employer Responses

Employers try many excuses to evade their obligations to supply information. Here are some that the NLRB has denied:

- "The union can get the information from employees."[159]
- "The request is too large."[160]
- "The grievance has no merit."[161]
- "The information has been posted."[162]
- "The grievance is not arbitrable."[163]
- "You can subpoena the information to the arbitration."[164]
- "Past grievances were resolved without this information."[165]
- "The materials are privileged."[166]

Confidentiality. An employer defense that is sometimes successful is *confidentiality*. This defense can only be used to protect information or records which are *particularly sensitive*. Employee medical records, psychological data, and aptitude test scores are usually considered confidential by the NLRB.[167] Company records disclosing trade secrets or containing sensitive research data have also been deemed confidential.[168] To invoke the confidentiality defense, an employer must have an established policy barring disclosure and must have consistently adhered to that policy.

An employer that asserts confidentiality must be willing to bargain with the union to attempt to accommodate the union's needs.[169] If medical confidentiality is asserted, for example, the union might agree to allow the employer to delete medical references from personnel files or delete employee names. If trade secrecy is raised, the union can offer to sign an agreement promising not to disclose the information.

Deadlines

The NLRB does not impose a uniform deadline for answering information requests. Employers must respond "promptly" but the acceptable time period depends on the amount of information requested and the difficulty in obtaining it. Items such as attendance records should be produced in one or two weeks.[170] Unreasonable delay is just as much an NLRA violation as outright refusal.

NLRB Charges

The employer's obligation to furnish grievance information runs solely to the union. Individual employees, including grievants, do not have legal standing to file information-request charges at the NLRB.[171] Stewards may file NLRB charges, but should always obtain approval from their chief steward, union president, or business agent. See below for a sample charge.

Sample Description of Violation for NLRB Charge Form ("Basis of Charge")

Since on or about September 29, 1994, the employer has failed and refused to provide the union with information requested in letters dated September 3, 1994 and September 10, 1994 which is necessary and relevant to the processing of a grievance.

QUESTIONS AND ANSWERS

1. Requesting information before filing grievance

Q. We believe that the company is not making its proper contributions (based on hours worked) to the union pension plan. Can we request company records *before* filing a grievance?

A. Yes. The union has a right to police its contract. When it has a reasonable basis for suspicion, it is entitled to information to make sure that the contract is being followed. Ask for records showing hours worked and payments made to the pension plan.[172]

2. Must the union specify the grievance that it is investigating?

Q. Our contract requires the employer to ensure that subcontractors pay wages and benefits equal to contract rates. We have asked the employer for a list of each of its subcontractors and the wages and benefits paid on each project. The employer is refusing to comply unless we tell it the specific jobs we are concerned about. Do we have to reveal our potential grievance?

A. No. A union does not have to reveal its grievance when making an information request. According to the Board, a union is "under no obligation to inform the [employer] of the specific nature of the grievance prior to obtaining the requested information."[173]

3. Personnel files

Q. Two employees were in a fight, but only one was disciplined. We asked for the personnel files of both workers. The company refuses to give us the file of the worker who was not disciplined unless we obtain his written authorization. Aren't we entitled to these records?

A. Yes. The personnel files of both employees are relevant to the grievance and must be turned over to the union. Unless the file contains sensitive medical data, you cannot be required to obtain the employee's consent.[174]

4. Attendance records

Q. After an employee was suspended for absenteeism, I asked for the attendance records of all employees in her department. The personnel manager said I could have the records of the grievant, but he could not release the records of other employees because many of them contain medical information relating to the reasons for absences. What are the union's rights?

A. An employer can refuse to disclose records containing medical information if it has a consistently enforced medical privacy policy. If that is the case, you may want to modify your request to allow the personnel manager to block out medical references in the records. If you make such an offer, the personnel manager will have no legal basis to withhold the records.[175]

5. Charging the union

Q. We requested the personnel files of four employees. The company insists that we pay $5 for clerical time and $5 for photocopy expenses in advance. Do we have to comply?

A. Not necessarily. According to the NLRB, the employer must bear the cost of supplying information — unless it can show that "substantial" costs are involved.[176] $10 is not substantial.

Note: If substantial costs are involved, the employer must bargain over the amount to be paid by the union. If the parties cannot come to an agreement, the union may request — and is entitled to — direct access to the records.[177] In other words, if the employer says it would take numerous clerical hours to review files, and refuses to absorb a reasonable share of the expense, the union can offer to do the work itself in company offices (under company supervision). Then see if the company provides the information!

6. Photocopies

Q. Is the union entitled to make photocopies of records we request?

A. This depends on the quantity of the requested material. If the relevant documents or entries are very brief, the employer can restrict the union to reading the material and taking notes by hand. But if the material is "voluminous", and it would be a burden to insist on hand notes, the employer must provide photocopies or allow the union to make them.[178]

7. Form of information

Q. For an overtime case, we asked the company for a list of hours worked by employees over the past six months. The company said that it would supply us with the time cards (over 1,000) and we would have to make our own computations. Is this sufficient?

A. Yes. An employer does not have to produce information in the precise form requested by the union.[179] But, if the company has *already computed* the data in question, it must produce it rather than put the union through unnecessary work.

8. Second request

Q. We made an information request and received several documents. Can we make a second request based on what we learned from the first batch?

A. Yes.

9. Information rights limited by contract?

Q. A clause in our collective-bargaining agreement permits the employer to conduct yearly performance appraisals. It further states that the union must obtain the written consent of an employee to see his or her appraisals. In the event of a grievance, does this restrict our NLRA right to see employee records?

A. Not necessarily. The NLRB rarely rules that a contract waives a union's right to grievance information. This is especially true when the restrictive language is not found in the grievance section of the collective-bargaining agreement.[180] If you file an NLRB charge, you should be able to get the appraisals without having to obtain employee consents.

10. "Too great a burden"

Q. For a safety grievance, we asked for information about machine malfunctions over the past five years.

The company is refusing on the grounds that the time needed to assemble the information would be too great a burden. Is this excuse recognized?

A. No. The NLRB does not recognize limits to an employer's obligation to provide relevant information. In one case involving a large bargaining unit, a company was ordered to supply information concerning hiring, seniority, job classifications, and promotions despite a claim that the request would entail almost 20,000 hours of clerical work! The NLRB ordered the parties to bargain on the union's share of the costs.[181]

11. Information needed for arbitration

Q. Arbitration is scheduled for next month. Is it too late to request information?

A. No. The duty to furnish information applies to arbitration proceedings.[182]

12. Information about non-bargaining-unit employees

Q. An employee was fired for being absent without calling in. The company has a plant-wide rule on this, but it is not as strict with the engineering employees as with union members. Can we ask for the personnel files of engineering employees we know have been guilty of the offense?

A. Yes. A union can request information about non-bargaining-unit employees as long as it can show relevance to a grievance. In your case, the disciplinary records of the engineering employees are relevant in determining whether the call-in rule is applied uniformly throughout the company.[183]

13. Information about supervisors

Q. An employee was suspended for on-site gambling. Can we ask for the personnel files of a supervisor who did the same thing last year?

A. Yes. Unions may request personnel files and other disciplinary information about supervisors if (1) supervisors are subject to the *same rules* as bargaining-unit members and (2) the union has a factual basis (such as a witness) for its allegation of similar misconduct.[184]

Note: Arbitrators often reverse discipline when supervisors get special treatment.[185]

14. Aptitude tests

Q. We are grieving a promotion decision that did not follow seniority. We asked for the personnel files of employees who applied for the position. The company says the records contain test scores. Can it refuse our request on the grounds of confidentiality?

A. Not completely. It must turn over the personnel files but not necessarily the aptitude test scores. Aptitude test scores are usually considered confidential. They are protected from disclosure if the company has a consistent policy of keeping them secret.[186]

15. Bringing in outside expert

Q. To support a time-study grievance, can we bring in a union expert to analyze the job?

A. Usually, yes. Under NLRB rules, unions can bring in outside experts, such as time-study specialists or industrial hygienists, to conduct studies or tests to support a grievance. Access to the worksite can be denied only if the employer establishes that the union can obtain the necessary information without entry or that the expert's presence will unduly interfere with operations.[187]

16. Witness name

Q. An employee was fired for leaving work early. Management says it has a witness from the bargaining unit. Does management have to reveal his or her name?

A. Yes. Employers must inform the union of the names (and addresses) of witnesses to an incident whether the witnesses are employees, supervisors, or customers.[188] Names of witnesses can be withheld only if (1) there is a history or likelihood of union intimidation of witnesses,[189] or (2) the employer has promised the witness confidentiality in terms of revealing the witness's name.[190]

Note: Even when an employer is allowed to keep secret an informant's name, it must give the union a summary of the information furnished by the informant.[191]

17. Witness statements

Q. The labor relations manager has given us the names of two employees who she says have given statements against an employee accused of stealing. Are we entitled to see the statements?

A. No. In a poorly reasoned 1974 decision, the NLRB carved out a disclosure exception for witness statements.[192]

18. Salaries

Q. We work for a TV station. Our collective-bargaining agreement allows management to negotiate separate personal-service contracts with "on-air" employees.

Does the union have a right to know the salary levels that are negotiated?

A. Yes. Salary information must be disclosed even if the employees wish to keep their incomes secret. The union has a right to see the contracts.[193]

19. Trade secrets

Q. We are considering filing a safety grievance and have asked for the names of all chemicals used in the mixing department. The company has refused, saying this would reveal "trade secrets." How can we get this information?

A. A union investigating health hazards is entitled to the generic and trade names of plant chemicals, with the sole exception of chemicals whose identity conveys valuable proprietary information (i.e., trade secrets)[194]. A union can usually get the names of even these substances if it offers to sign a "trade secrecy agreement" promising to keep the information confidential among particular union representatives.[195]

20. New employees

Q. Does the company have to respond to a union request for the telephone numbers of new employees?

A. Yes. The union can also request job locations, hours of work, addresses, job classifications, and starting salaries.[196]

21. Internal company study

Q. In the midst of a subcontracting grievance, we learned that, prior to contacting the work out, the company hired a consultant to study the issue. Do we have a right to see the report?

A. Yes. Company studies that are relevant to a grievance must be disclosed to the union. If the the report contains sensitive information, the union may be required to sign a "confidentiality agreement" promising not to disclose the report to others.[197]

22. Security report

Q. An employee was discharged for damaging company property. The company has a detailed security report. Can we request it?

A. Yes. As a general rule, investigative, security, and supervisory reports must be disclosed to the union.[198] However, since a Board rule insulates witness statements from disclosure, the security report does not have to be provided in full if it contains verbatim accounts of witness interviews. If it contains summaries of conversations, or reports of statements, and if the witnesses were not promised confidentiality, the full report must be supplied.[199]

23. Sales records

Q. The company says it is laying off employees in the shipping department because of poor sales. We think the real reason is to eliminate militant union members. Are we entitled to see the sales records?

A. Yes. In a similar case the NLRB ordered a company to provide: (1) a list of customers; (2) the accounts payable journal; (3) invoices from suppliers; (4) check-books; (5) the general ledger; (6) the general journal; (7) the chart of accounts; and (8) computer summary sheets.[200]

24. Handwriting analysis

Q. An employee was discharged for allegedly falsifying a doctor's signature on a sickness and accident form. The company claims it has a professional handwriting analysis demonstrating a forgery. When we asked for the analysis, the company refused, saying we could hire our own expert. Do we have a right to see the company's analysis?

A. Yes. A handwriting analysis is not a confidential document. It must be turned over to the union.[201]

25. Affirmative action plan

Q. We are pursuing a sex discrimination grievance for six female employees denied promotions. Our employer is a federal contractor and we know it has an affirmative action plan which analyzes the workforce by race and sex and lists hiring and promotion goals. Can we demand a copy of the plan to help us prepare the grievance?

A. You should ask for the plan, but you may not get all of it. According to NLRB and court decisions, a union investigating discrimination is entitled to the workforce-analysis portion of an employer's affirmative action plan.[202] But the union may not be entitled to the rest of the plan, including the employer's goals and commitments. Production of this material would, according to one court decision, discourage an employer from engaging in frank self-critical analysis.[203]

Note: Unions may be able to get entire affirmative action plans through the federal Freedom of Information Act (FOIA). FOIA requests can be made to the Office of Federal Contract Compliance Programs (OFCCP), the agency to which federal contractors must submit affirmative action plans.

26. Plant closing information

Q. Our employer has decided to close our plant. Are we entitled to documents that could help us to argue against the decision?

A. Probably not. According to the U.S. Supreme Court, a decision to close a business, or a part of a business, purely for economic reasons, is not a mandatory subject of bargaining.[204] Therefore, there is no basis for a union demand for information on the closure decision.[205]

Note: A decision to move a facility is a different matter. This decision is likely to be classified as a mandatory subject of bargaining — giving the union the right to request information bearing on the decision.[206]

Further note: The *effect* of a closure decision is a mandatory bargaining subject.[207] Unions may submit information requests relating to issues such as employee transfers, health insurance, pensions, and severance benefits.

27. Expired contract

Q. Our collective-bargaining agreement expired two months ago. We are working without a contract. Last week an employee was discharged in my department. I intend to pursue a grievance although I am told that after contract expiration we are not entitled to arbitration. Am I entitled to information from the company concerning the grievance?

A. Yes. Union information rights continue after a contract expires.[208] Management must meet and bargain with you on the grievance.

28. Employee wants his personnel file

Q. An employee I represent wants me to get him his personnel file. Do I have an automatic right to his file under NLRA rules?

A. No. Under the NLRA, stewards have rights to personnel files only as part of a grievance investigation. Employees with a curiosity to see their files must look to state laws. Several states require employers, both union and non-union, to show personnel files to employees on request.

29. Privacy Act

Q. We work for the Postal Service. When we requested employee personnel files for a grievance, our manager said he could not give them to the union because of the U.S. Privacy Act. Is he right?

A. No. The U.S. Privacy Act restricts disclosure of certain data held by federal agencies and federal contractors.[209] But the NLRB has ruled that this law does not affect union rights to grievance-related information under the NLRA.[210]

30. Employer request

Q. We are going to arbitration to try to get full-time status for two employees who have worked the contract minimum of 600 hours. Management is asking for our time computations. Do we have to give up this information?

A. Yes. The duty to furnish information applies to unions. Unions must provide information an employer needs to evaluate a grievance or to prepare for arbitration.[211] Failure to respond may subject the union to unfair-labor-practice proceedings at the NLRB.

CHAPTER 5

"Weingarten Rights" (Union Representation During Investigatory Interviews)

A VITAL steward function is to prevent management from intimidating employees. Nowhere is this more important than in closed-door meetings when supervisors or guards, often trained in inter-rogation techniques, attempt to induce employees to confess to mistakes or wrongdoing.

The NLRA gives employees the right to assistance from union representatives during investigatory interviews. Although not explicit in the Act, the right was declared by the U.S. Supreme Court in 1975 in *NLRB v. J. Weingarten, Inc.*[212] The rules the Court announced are known as *Weingarten* rights.

Unions should encourage employees to assert their *Weingarten* rights. The presence of a steward can help in many ways:

- The steward can serve as a witness to prevent super-visors from giving a false account of the conversa-tion.
- The steward can object to intimidating tactics or con-fusing questions.
- The steward can, when appropriate, advise an em-ployee against blindly denying everything, thereby giving the appearance of dishonesty and guilt.

- The steward can help an employee to avoid making fatal admissions.
- The steward can warn an employee against losing his or her temper.
- The steward can raise extenuating factors.

What is an Investigatory Interview?

Weingarten rights apply during investigatory interviews. An investigatory interview occurs when: (1) management *questions an employee* to obtain information; and (2) the employee has a *reasonable belief that discipline or other adverse consequences may result* from what he or she says. Investigatory interviews relate to such subjects as:

- absenteeism
- accidents
- compliance with work rules
- damage to company property
- drinking
- drugs
- falsification of records
- fighting
- insubordination
- lateness
- poor attitude
- poor work performance
- sabotage
- slowdowns
- theft
- violation of safety rules

Shop-floor conversations. Not every discussion with management is an investigatory interview. For example, a supervisor may speak to an employee about the proper way to do a job. Even if the supervisor asks the employee questions, this is not an investigatory interview because the possibility of discipline is remote.

A routine conversation changes character if a supervisor becomes dissatisfied with an employee's answers and takes a hostile attitude. If this happens, the meeting becomes an investigatory interview and *Weingarten* applies.

Disciplinary announcements. When a supervisor calls an employee to the office to announce a warning or other discipline, is this an investigatory interview? The NLRB says no, because the supervisor is merely informing the employee of a previously arrived-at decision.[213] Such a meeting becomes an investigatory interview, however, if the supervisor asks questions that are related to the subject matter of the discipline.

Employee Rights

Under the Supreme Court's *Weingarten* decision, when an investigatory interview occurs, these rules apply:

- The employee may request union representation before or during the interview.
- After the request, the employer must choose from among three options:
  1. Grant the request and delay questioning until the union representative arrives.
  2. Deny the request and end the interview immediately.
  3. Give the employee a choice of: (a) having the interview without representation (usually a mistake) or (b) ending the interview.
- If the employer denies the request for union representation, and questions the employee, it commits an unfair labor practice and the employee *may refuse to answer.*

Steward Rights

Supervisors sometime assert that the only function of a steward at an investigatory interview is to observe the discussion; in other words to be a silent witness. This is wrong. The steward has the right to counsel the employee during the interview and to assist the employee to present the facts. Legal cases have established the following rights and obligations:

- When the steward arrives, the supervisor must inform the employee and the steward of the subject matter of the interview: for example, the type of misconduct which is being investigated. (The supervisor does not, however, have to reveal management's entire case.)[214]

- The steward can take the employee aside for a private pre-interview conference before questioning begins.[215]
- The steward can speak during the interview. (But, the steward has no right to bargain over the purpose of the interview[216] or to obstruct the interview.[217])
- The steward can interrupt to object to a question[218] or request that the supervisor clarify a question so that the employee can understand what is being asked.[219]
- The steward can advise the employee not to answer questions that are abusive, misleading, badgering, confusing, or harassing.[220]
- When the questioning ends, the steward can provide information to justify the employee's conduct.[221]

Educating Members

Employees sometime confuse the *Weingarten* rules with the *Miranda* rules. Under the U.S. Supreme Court's *Miranda* decision, police who question criminal suspects in custody must notify them of their right to remain silent and to have a lawyer present.[222] Unfortunately, the Supreme Court did not impose similar requirements in its *Weingarten* decision. Employers have no obligations to inform employees of their rights to union representation. *This is the union's job.*

Unions should explain *Weingarten* rights at union meetings and in newsletters. Consider distributing wallet-sized cards saying the following:

> (If called to a meeting with management, read the following to management or present the card before the meeting starts.)
>
> If this discussion could in any way lead to my being disciplined or terminated, or affect my personal working conditions, I respectfully request that my union representative, officer, or steward be present at this meeting. Without representation present, I choose not to participate in this discussion.

NLRB Charges

Failure to adhere to the *Weingarten* rules is an unfair labor practice. NLRB charges should be filed if employers disregard requests for union assistance or interfere with stewards' rights. Charges are not deferred unless the union has a *Weingarten*-rights clause in its contract. Violations are rarely considered "de minimis".[223] See below for a sample charge.

Sample Description of Violation for NLRB Charge Form ("Basis of Charge")

> On October 1, 1994, the employer refused the request of employee Harold Brown for union representation during an investigatory interview.

QUESTIONS AND ANSWERS

1. Request to attend meeting

Q. I am a department steward. If I see a worker being questioned in a supervisor's office, can I ask to attend the meeting?

A. Yes. A steward has a protected right to request admission to such a meeting.[224] If the meeting is routine, the request can be denied. But if the meeting is an investigatory interview, the employee must be allowed to indicate whether the steward's presence is desired.[225]

2. Coercing employee to drop request

Q. An employee, summoned to an interview with his supervisor, asked for his steward. In response, the supervisor said, "You can request your steward, but if you do, I will have to bring in the plant manager, and you know how temperamental she is. If we can keep it at this level, things will be better for you." Violation?

A. Yes. The supervisor is raising the specter of discipline to coerce the employee into abandoning his *Weingarten* rights. This is an unfair labor practice.[226]

3. Can employee refuse to go to meeting?

Q. An employee was ordered by her manager to go to the personnel office for a "talk" about her attendance. She asked to bring her steward but the manager said she would have to make this request when she got to the office. Can the employee refuse to go to the personnel office without her steward?

A. No. *Weingarten* rights do not arise until the interview begins. The employee must go to the office and make her request to the person conducting the interview.[227] An employee can refuse to go to a meeting only if a supervisor makes clear in advance that union representation will be denied.[228]

4. Medical examination

Q. Our company requires medical examinations for recalled employees out of work three months or more. Do the employees have a right to a steward during the examination?

A. No. Medical examinations are not investigatory interviews. *Weingarten* rights do not apply.[229]

5. Lie detector test

Q. Do *Weingarten* rights apply to polygraph examinations?

A. Yes. An employee has a right to union assistance during the pre-examination interview and the polygraph examination.[230]

6. Drug test

Q. If management asks an employee to submit to a urine test for drugs, does *Weingarten* apply?

A. Partly. When no questioning takes place, a urine test is not an investigatory interview and an employee does not have a right to the presence of a steward. Management must, however, allow the employee to consult with a union representative to decide whether or not to take the test.[231]

7. Locker search

Q. If management orders an employee to open a locker, can the employee insist on a steward being present?

A. Not necessarily. Locker, car, or handbag searches are not investigatory interviews. An employee does not have a right to insist on the presence of a steward unless a guard or supervisor asks the employee questions.[232]

8. Counselling session

Q. An employee was given a written warning for poor attendance and told she must participate in absence-counselling with the personnel department. Does she have a right to a union steward at the counselling sessions?

A. This depends on whether the employee has a fear that the counselling sessions could result in further discipline. For example, if notes from the sessions are kept in the employee's permanent record, or if other employees have been disciplined for speaking up at counselling sessions, the employee's fears would be reasonable and would entitle her to steward.[233] But if the personnel representative gives firm assurances that the meetings will not be used for further discipline, and promises that the conversations will remain confidential, *Weingarten* rights probably would not apply.[234]

9. Warning slip

Q. Supervisors in our shop give warning slips for misconduct and ask employees to sign copies to acknowledge receipt. Does an employee have a *Weingarten* right to consult a steward before signing?

A. No. If a supervisor does not ask questions, *Weingarten* does not apply.[235]

10. Request for private attorney

Q. Can a worker insist on the presence of an attorney before answering questions at an investigatory interview?

A. No. The *Weingarten* rules only provide for the assistance of union representatives.[236]

11. Telephone interview

Q. Over the weekend, a supervisor called a worker at home to ask questions about missing tools. Did the worker have to answer the questions?

A. No. *Weingarten* rights apply to telephone interviews.[237] An employee who fears discipline can refuse to answer questions until he or she has a chance to consult with a union representative.

12. Disciplinary announcement

Q. An employee was called into the plant manager's office. She asked for her steward, but her request was ignored. The manager said, "Doreen, yesterday you violated a supervisor's order. We are giving you a one-day suspension for insubordination." Did the company violate *Weingarten*?

A. No. *Weingarten* rights do not apply to a meeting where an employer simply announces discipline.[238]

13. Steward not at worksite

Q. If an employee's steward is out sick, can the employee insist that an interview be delayed until the steward comes to work?

A. No. Management does not have to delay its investigation if another union representative is available to assist the employee.[239]

14. Investigation of steward

Q. I am a steward. If I am called in by my supervisor to discuss a problem with my work, can I bring my chief steward?

A. Yes. Stewards have the same *Weingarten* rights as other employees. If you have a fear of discipline or other adverse consequences, you are entitled to assistance.[240]

15. Shop meeting

Q. If management calls a meeting to lecture employees about job performance, do employees have a right to bring a union representative to the meeting?

A. Not necessarily. A meeting that does not involve interrogation is not an investigatory interview.[241] *Weingarten* rights do not apply unless management asks questions of employees in a manner that creates a reasonable fear of discipline.

16. Remedies for Weingarten violations

Q. If management rejects an employee's request for union assistance, questions the employee, gets the employee to confess to wrongdoing, and fires the employee, will the NLRB order the employee reinstated because of the *Weingarten* violation?

A. Probably not. The NLRB used to order reinstatement with back pay for employees who were fired as a result of admissions during an illegally conducted *Weingarten* interview.[242] But in 1984 the Reagan-appointed NLRB ruled that such a remedy was an unwarranted "windfall" for employees.[243] The standard *Weingarten* penalty is now a bulletin-board posting in which the employer acknowledges that it violated the *Weingarten* rules and promises to obey them in the future.

Note: The remedy is different for employees discharged for exercising a *Weingarten* right such as requesting a steward or refusing to answer questions when a request is denied. In such cases, the NLRB imposes a "make-whole" remedy, including reinstatement and back pay.[244]

17. Recording the interview

Q. Can a supervisor tape record an investigatory interview?

A. Possibly. Nothing in the *Weingarten* decision prevents an employer from tape recording an investigatory interview. However, if this represents a new employer policy, the steward should object on the grounds that the union should have received prior notice of the new policy and an opportunity to bargain about it.[245]

18. Can employee select a particular representative?

Q. If an employee asks to be represented by her chief steward instead of her department steward, must management comply?

A. Yes. If two representatives are equally available, an employee's request for a particular representative must be honored.[246]

19. Employee asked to inform on others

Q. An employee was summoned to a meeting and asked about the involvement of other employees in illegal activities. Could he have insisted on the presence of a union representative?

A. Yes. Although the employee may not be involved in wrongdoing himself, he risks discipline if he refuses to inform on others or admits that he was aware of illegal activities. Because what he says or doesn't say at the meeting could get him into trouble, he is entitled to representation.

CHAPTER 6

Mid-term Changes: The Obligation to Bargain

UNION representatives, including stewards, must be knowledgeable about NLRA mid-term (mid-contract) bargaining rules. In many cases, these rules require employers to bargain with unions before implementing new rules, job practices, and work assignments.

The Bargaining Duty

Section 8(a)(5) of the NLRA requires employers to bargain collectively with unions. The application of this principle to contract negotiations is well known. But Section 8(a)(5) also applies during the term of a collective-bargaining agreement — if the employer should decide to make changes in matters not fixed by the contract.

Under NLRB doctrine, an employer violates Section 8(a)(5) if it changes or enacts new terms or conditions of employment without (1) *notifying the union* well in advance of the proposed changes; and (2) giving the union an *adequate opportunity to bargain* prior to implementation.[247]

Changes affecting wages, hours, or other terms of employment that are made without notice or bargaining are called *unilateral changes*. They are unfair labor practices — even if the employer has a good reason for its actions.

Unions may file NLRB charges within six months of a unilateral change. The NLRB can order the employer to rescind the rule or practice and compensate employees for any lost wages or benefits. The NLRB can also order the reinstatement, with back pay, of employees who are suspended or discharged for violating unilaterally imposed work rules.

Note: The NLRB often defers unilateral-change charges to the grievance and arbitration process (usually to get an interpretation of a management-rights clause). However, when unilateral-change charges are combined with failure-to-provide-information charges, deferral can sometimes be avoided (see this chapter, question 18).

Sample Description of Violation for NLRB Charge Form ("Basis of Charge")

On June 19, 1994, the employer unilaterally changed the working conditions of bargaining-unit employees by implementing a new policy prohibiting employees from wearing shorts. The union requested bargaining prior to implementation but the employer ignored the union's request.

Which Changes Must Be Bargained?

Under NLRB rules, the mid-term bargaining obligation applies only to new rules or job practices that have a *material, substantial, or significant impact* on employees.[248] Changing the workload of a single employee does not require bargaining. But increasing the workload of several employees, or an entire department, triggers the bargaining obligation. An employer can unilaterally substitute a time clock for a written sign-in procedure. But changing shift starting times must be bargained.

Bargaining categories. The NLRB recognizes two major categories of bargaining subjects: mandatory and voluntary. As a concession to employers, the NLRB limits the bargaining obligation to mandatory subjects. Mandatory subjects include changes in wages, hours, and benefits as well as other changes which directly

Mandatory Subjects

(may not be changed without prior notice to the union and bargaining on request)

- absence rules
- automation decisions
- bathroom procedures
- bonus programs
- clean-up rules
- disciplinary procedures or penalties
- dress codes
- drug/alcohol testing
- elimination of positions
- employee privileges (such as right to listen to radios, receive telephone calls, smoke, etc.)
- employee purchase plan rules
- evaluation systems
- food service hours
- free coffee

- grievance procedures
- grooming standards
- insurance plans
- layoffs for economic reasons
- "light duty" policies
- meal or coffee break rules
- new hours or shifts
- new positions
- outside conduct rules
- outside employment rules
- parking rules
- pay check procedures
- pay rates
- physical examinations
- production quotas
- relocation of bargaining-unit work (generally)

affect the terms or conditions of employment. Voluntary subjects (for which bargaining is not required) include managerial prerogatives such as supervisor selection, production methods, and plant closing decisions. The following are among the subjects that have been classified by the NLRB:

(Mandatory Subjects continued)

- safety awards
- safety and health rules
- smoking rules
- subcontracting decisions
- tardiness rules
- time off prior to holidays
- transfer of bargaining-unit work to non-bargaining-unit employees
- union steward and officer privileges (such as paid leaves, access to facilities, time off, etc.)
- vacation policies
- wages
- workloads
- work rules

Voluntary Subjects

(may be changed without notice or bargaining)

- decisions to close plants or eliminate departments
- general business practices such as choice of advertising or financial arrangements
- hiring practices (non-discriminatory)
- pre-employment testing procedures
- production methods
- relocation decisions accompanied by basic changes in the employer's operation
- selection of supervisors

Note: Any subjects which are included in the collective-bargaining agreement are fixed for the term of the agreement and cannot be changed without union consent even if the employer offers to bargain.

Bargaining Rules

The following NLRB rules apply to changes in mandatory subjects:

1. The employer must give the union prior notice that a change is planned. The notice must be given sufficiently in advance to allow the union a meaningful opportunity to bargain.
2. After receiving notice of the planned change, the union must make a request to bargain prior to implementation. The request must be submitted even if the employer has announced its plans in a positive manner or otherwise gives the appearance that its mind is made up. If the union fails to act with diligence, it loses its bargaining rights.

   Note: Filing a grievance does not suffice as a request to bargain. A separate bargaining request must be submitted. Put the request in writing and keep a copy.
3. After receiving the union's request, the employer must suspend implementation of the new rule or practice and must agree to meet with the union to bargain on the change.
4. Bargaining must be conducted in good faith with the intention of reaching agreement. The employer must permit sufficient meetings to be held and must provide relevant information requested by the union.

5. Bargaining must continue until agreement is reached or the parties come to *impasse* (a good-faith dead-lock). If negotiations come to impasse, the employer can implement its proposed change (and the union can grieve).

    Note: Don't fall into the trap of going to the first bargaining session, rejecting the employer's proposal, and walking out. This only helps the employer to declare impasse. By asking for further meetings, making detailed requests for information, and submitting written counter-proposals, you can extend the bargaining process and perhaps persuade the employer to withdraw its proposal or agree to a middle ground.

Sample Bargaining Request

To: Vinnie Lamothe
From: John Merlo, President Local 150
Subject: Union request for bargaining
Date: July 15, 1994

The union hereby requests bargaining concerning the company's recent announcement concerning the use of hearing protection devices.
Please suspend any planned implementation of the new rule and advise the union regarding the time(s) and place(s) at which the company will be able and willing to negotiate regarding the above-mentioned proposed change.

Sincerely yours,

John Merlo

Management-Rights Clauses

Employers often argue that contractual "management-rights" clauses permit them to make mid-term changes without bargaining. Management-rights clauses usually set out an employer's right to direct the enterprise, make rules, and assign work. Under NLRB doctrine, however, a management-rights clause constitutes a waiver of bargaining rights only if it "clearly and unmistakably" states a union's intention to give up its rights.[249] A clause saying that management has the "exclusive" authority to adopt safety rules may be a bargaining waiver for such rules. But more general expressions of managerial rights, as are found in many collective-bargaining agreements, do not reach the waiver status.[250] Moreover, NLRB doctrine holds that the failure of a union to request bargaining on past changes in work rules or job practices does not create a waiver and eliminate the union's right to demand bargaining on future changes.[251]

Note: A union that is concerned that its contractual management-rights clause may be construed as a bargaining waiver should try to obtain new contract language, perhaps by adding a sentence affirming that the union is not waiving its rights to bargain. If this is not practicable, consider submitting a letter to management during contract negotiations stating that the union does not view the existing management-rights clause as a waiver of its NLRA bargaining rights. This puts the burden on the employer to strengthen the clause or perhaps lose its waiver defense.

QUESTIONS AND ANSWERS

1. Sick-leave rule

Q. Last week, without notice to the union, the company announced that anyone out sick for two days or longer must submit a doctor's note. Is the rule legal?

A. No. Sick-leave rules are mandatory bargaining subjects.[252] Unless a management-rights or other contract clause clearly permits the company to adopt sick-leave rules without bargaining, the employer must give the union prior notice and adequate opportunity to bargain. File an unfair-labor-practice charge at the NLRB.

2. Dress code

Q. After a new manager was hired, he announced that employees will no longer be allowed to wear shorts at work. When we asked to bargain, he refused to meet. Is the new policy enforceable?

A. Not legally. Dress codes and appearance standards are mandatory bargaining subjects.[253] The refusal to bargain makes the new rule unlawful.

3. Bathroom procedure

Q. Five months ago, the company unilaterally adopted a rule requiring employees to get permission before going to the bathroom. Two employees have been disciplined for ignoring the rule. Can this discipline stick?

A. No. Bathroom procedures must be bargained.[254] Discipline based on the unilaterally-imposed rule is illegal. Make sure your NLRB charges are filed within six months of the rule's implementation.[255]

4. Workload

Q. A housekeeping employee in our union is responsible for cleaning offices on two floors. Yesterday, her supervisor told her she would be responsible for part of a third floor as well. The union was not notified. Is this a unilateral-change violation?

A. No. Workload changes that affect only one employee do not have a sufficient impact on the bargaining unit to require bargaining prior to implementation.[256] Depending on contract language, however, a contract grievance may be possible.

5. Drug testing

Q. Does an employer have to bargain before instituting a drug testing policy?

A. Yes. A drug or alcohol testing policy is a significant employment condition. Employers must bargain on request over such issues as the nature of the test, the purposes for which it can be used, and the consequences of a refusal to take the test.[257] Unions should request extensive information to assist them in bargaining.

6. Food prices

Q. Does management have to give the union an oppor-tunity to bargain before raising food prices in the com-pany cafeteria?

A. No. Although food prices are a mandatory subject of bargaining, the NLRB has a special rule. Employers do not have to bargain prior to raising prices, but must be willing to negotiate afterwards. The bargaining obliga-tion applies even if the cafeteria is run by an outside vendor, since the employer is in a position either to influence price levels or to make up for increases.[258]

7. Safety rule

Q. Can the company adopt a new safety rule without agreeing to bargain?

A. No. Safety rules are mandatory subjects.[259]

8. Tightening up enforcement

Q. Company rules specify two 15-minute breaks. For years, however, all employees have been permitted to take breaks for 20 minutes. Last week, the company announced it was tightening up. Five workers were cited for being late and one was suspended for two infractions. Was the company required to bargain with the union before it began its strict enforcement?

A. Yes. In 1996 the NLRB clarified this issue, saying that an employer establishes a term and condition of employ-ment by consistently failing to enforce a work rule over several years. If the employer decides to change course and apply the rule strictly, it must give the union prior notice and must bargain if the union requests.[260]

In your case, the change to strict enforcement of the 15-minute policy appears to have violated the rule against unilateral changes. Discipline imposed pursuant to the policy is invalid and must be rescinded.[261]

9. Union privilege

Q. For years, management has allowed the union to use the labor relations photocopy machine to copy grievances and other documents. Last month, without any bargaining, the practice was stopped because we are "using the machine too much." Is this legal?

A. No. Union privileges, such as the use of employer photocopy machines, telephones, or office space, are mandatory bargaining subjects.[262] Prior notice and bargaining to agreement or impasse must occur before they can be taken away.

10. Union business

Q. Although our contract is silent on the subject, our company has always allowed stewards time off work to investigate grievances. But last week the company announced that stewards would only be able to do union business during their breaks and at lunch time. Didn't it have to bargain on this?

A. Yes. Rules restricting union business time are mandatory bargaining subjects.[263]

11. Grievance procedures

Q. For years we have held grievance meetings with management during the work day. Yesterday, labor relations announced that supervisors did not have enough time and from now on the meetings would have to be

held after working hours. Can the company do this without bargaining?

A. No. Rules relating to the time and conduct of grievance meetings are mandatory bargaining subjects.[264]

12. Subcontract

Q. In the middle of the contract, the company hired an
outside firm to perform painting previously handled by
union maintenance personnel. Didn't the company have
to bargain on this?

A. Yes. Under NLRB doctrine, if a subcontracting decision substitutes non-bargaining-unit employees for bargaining-unit employees doing the same work, with no
change in the scope or direction of the enterprise, the
employer must give notice and bargain on request prior
to implementation.[265]

13. Light-duty policy

Q. Our company met with its workers' compensation
insurer to reduce costs. They worked out a new program
that requires employees to accept temporary light duty —
without regard to classification — after an injury. Can the
company implement the program without bargaining?

A. No. Light-duty programs are mandatory subjects.[266]
Unions should demand bargaining on the scope of the
program, duration, pay, and the penalty for refusing to
take part.

14. Business emergency

Q. We work for a telephone answering service that is
open 24 hours a day, seven days a week. Two days before

Easter, three operators quit. The company handled the problem at the last minute by establishing a procedure for Easter staffing that was markedly different than the procedure in previous years. Did the company violate the law by failing to give the union an opportunity to bargain?

A. Not necessarily. The NLRB recognizes a limited right to take action without bargaining when an emergency requires an employer to act quickly.[267]

Note: The business emergency defense is not met simply by a need to save money. According to the NLRB, "only in extraordinary situations will this exception apply."[268]

15. Fait accompli

Q. Last month, management unilaterally adopted a rule forbidding beards. When we protested to the personnel director, she said she would bargain but the new rule would apply in the meantime. Is this sufficient?

A. No. An employer cannot escape its obligations by agreeing to bargain on a subject after a unilateral change is in place. This is called a *fait accompli*. It gives the employer an unfair advantage in any subsequent bargaining. NLRB policy requires employers to suspend policies prior to bargaining.[269] If the personnel director refuses, file a unilateral-change charge at the NLRB.

16. Change mandated by law

Q. Our company announced a smoking ban and refuses to meet with the union. Labor relations says that it can do this because a new city law bans smoking in workplaces. Can the company avoid bargaining?

A. This depends. When a federal, state, or local law requires a change in employer policies, *and there is no discretion on how to apply the law*, an employer may comply with the law without bargaining.[270] In many cases, however, there is discretion on how to comply with a new law or regulation. In those situations, the union must be given prior notice and an opportunity to bargain.[271]

17. Contract expiration

Q. Our contract expires tomorrow. If we work without a contract, could our employer unilaterally reduce our wages or benefits?

A. This depends. If contract negotiations have reached impasse, the employer is permitted to implement changes that are consistent with its final bargaining position. But on non-impasse issues the obligation to bargain continues and, in fact, is usually stronger because employers cannot rely on management-rights clauses.[272]

18. Overcoming deferral

Q. Are there any ways to avoid NLRB deferral of uni-lateral-change charges?

A. One strategy, where the employer's actions warrant it, is to add an information-request charge. Under Board policy, if a meritorious information-request charge (which is never deferrable) is closely related to a meritorious unilateral-change charge, the regional director can include both charges in the complaint despite the employer's request for deferral.[273]

For example, if the employer announces a subcontract and refuses to bargain about it, submit a detailed request for information about the decision. If the employer fails to respond, or responds only in part, file an NLRB charge alleging an information refusal as well as a unilateral change.

19. Can a rank-and-file employee file a unilateral-change charge?

Q. Our employer has announced a new safety rule to which the union has no objection. Can a rank-and-file employee file a unilateral-change charge at the NLRB to try to block the rule?

A. No. Only the union and its representatives have standing to file unilateral-change charges at the NLRB.[274] If the union makes a good-faith judgment not to oppose a new policy or rule, individual members cannot force bargaining.

20. Using the grievance procedure to contest new policies

Q. Management has implemented a new drug testing policy. It bargained for two months, reached impasse,

and then adopted its original plan. Can we use the grievance procedure to continue to fight the policy?

A. Yes. There are three ways to grieve a new disciplinary policy:

If the new policy conflicts with a written contract provision, base the grievance on this provision. This is a
happy, but rare, occurrence.

In the absence of favorable contract language, consider filing a "past-practice grievance." Such a grievance
relies on the fact that arbitrators usually consider longstanding practices and customs, even though unwritten,
to be part and parcel of the collective-bargaining agreement. Past-practice grievances are more successful
when management is attempting to eliminate a valuable
employee benefit or union privilege. They do not work
well, however, when contesting new methods of operation, work procedures, or disciplinary policies.

A third possible approach is to file a grievance contending that the new policy violates the "rule of reason-
ableness." This is also a difficult grievance. You will
have to persuade an arbitrator that the drug testing policy lacks a rational justification or is extremely unfair in
the way it is applied.[275]

CHAPTER 7
Union Duty of Fair Representation

THIS CHAPTER considers the other side of the labor law coin: namely, the *union obligation* known as the duty of fair representation (DFR). This duty is not explicit in the NLRA, but the U.S. Supreme Court says that it flows from the privilege of exclusive representation granted to unions by the Act. A union violates the duty when its conduct in representing employees is "arbitrary, discriminatory, or in bad faith."[276]

Employees who fail to receive fair representation can file NLRB charges against the union. Employees can also sue in court. If the union is found guilty, judgment and litigation expenses can cost the union many thousands of dollars.

DFR Charges

Some duty-of-fair-representation charges are brought by employees who are upset with collective-bargaining agreements. But most DFR claims are filed by employees who are dissatisfied with the way their grievances have been handled. Unions may be charged with:
- Failing to file a grievance
- Failing to investigate a grievance
- Withdrawing a grievance
- Settling a grievance short of full relief
- Failing to take a grievance to arbitration

- Failing to prepare for arbitration
- Mishandling an arbitration

A dissatisfied employee must prove more than bad results or mistakes by the union. According to the NLRB, "Mere negligence, poor judgment, or ineptitude in grievance handling are insufficient to establish a breach of the duty of fair representation."[277] Although some Board and court decisions have found against unions on a showing of "perfunctory conduct," such as missing a grievance-filing deadline, or failing to investigate a grievance, generally an employee must show that the union's actions were based on *hostility or personal bias*. For example, a union violates the fair-representation duty if it refuses to file a grievance because an employee is an opponent of the union's leadership.

Decisions to file grievances, or to take cases to arbitration, may not be affected by a worker's race, gender, nationality, age, religion, politics, union membership, dues-paying status, or lack of popularity. The union must represent all members of the bargaining unit.

Union Liability

Most DFR charges are dismissed by the NLRB or the courts. However, when a union is found guilty, the financial impact can be enormous. One reason is a 1983 U.S. Supreme Court rule apportioning financial liability between unions and employers.[278] In the case of a discharge, a union that fails to arbitrate a meritorious case can be held responsible for back pay from the approximate date a hypothetical arbitrator's decision would have reinstated the employee. The following scenario explains the rule:

Steven Thomas, earning $20,000 a year, is discharged when a supervisor smells marijuana in his work area. The union grieves, but does not take the case to arbitration. The reason for the union's decision is that Thomas is a malcontent who led an attempt to decertify the union.

When Thomas learns that his grievance has been dropped, he sues the union and the company in federal court. Two years later, the company is found guilty of discharging Thomas without just cause because there was no first-hand evidence that Thomas was smoking marijuana. The union is found guilty of a DFR violation for discriminating against Thomas because of his decertification activities.

Thomas is awarded reinstatement and back pay. Because the judge finds that an arbitrator would have reinstated Thomas in six months, the company is ordered to pay $10,000 (one-half year's pay). The union is ordered to pay $30,000 (for the one and one-half year period from the projected arbitration award to the court-ordered reinstatement). Legal fees bring the union's expenses to over $50,000.

Racial, Ethnic, or Gender Discrimination

When an employee is a victim of racial, ethnic, or gender discrimination or harassment, the union must respond. A union may be charged with a fair-representation or civil rights violation if it fails to file a grievance or take other action.

Racial and ethnic discrimination includes segregated job assignments, name-calling, and ethnic jokes. Gender harassment includes lewd proposals, sexual jokes, ridicule, unwanted physical contact, and sexual assaults. Stewards must act whether the harassment comes from supervisors or from union members. When an employer or supervisor is at fault, the steward should assist the employee in filing federal or state civil rights charges in addition to submitting a contract grievance.

Precautions

It is obviously important for stewards to avoid conduct which could subject the union to a DFR charge. Here are some guidelines:

- When you are responsible for a grievance, conduct a full investigation. Interview the grievant and other witnesses. Request files, documents, and other relevant information. Record what you have done in a pocket diary.
- Do not refuse to process a grievance because of an employee's sex, race, nationality, age, religion, politics, personality, or non-dues-paying status. Adhere to contractual time limits. Diligently represent all employees in the bargaining unit — even if you consider the employee to be a destructive force within the union.
- Keep the employee informed of the progress of the grievance. Maintain a good relationship. If the union decides to drop or settle the grievance, advise the grievant in writing or in the presence of a witness, explain the reasons, and keep notes of the conversation. Inform the grievant of any procedures he or she may use to appeal the union's decision.
- Prepare thoroughly for grievance meetings. If a business agent or union attorney handles the case at arbitration, he or she should meet with the grievant well in advance of the hearing.

QUESTIONS AND ANSWERS

1. Far-fetched grievance

Q. It sounds as if a union must file a grievance whenever an employee complains — no matter how far-fetched the claim. Is this true?

A. No. The union does not have to file a grievance if it has a good-faith belief that the employee's claim is unfounded, cannot be won, or has no basis in the contract.[279]

2. Sexual harassment

Q. Several female employees have complained about sexual harassment by a supervisor. We have a non-discrimination clause in our contract, but I would rather not file a grievance because I am afraid the supervisor will get his back up and this will jeopardize other grievances. What should I do?

A. File a grievance! A union cannot hold back a legitimate grievance because it fears management's biased reactions. Failure to enforce the contract's prohibition against sexual discrimination could subject the union to DFR charges.[280]

3. Representing nonmembers

Q. As a steward, it galls me to represent employees who won't join the union. Can I tell these employees that it costs money to run a union and they should join if they want us to process their cases?

A. Be careful. The union has a legal duty to represent nonmembers. You cannot condition grievance processing on joining the union.[281]

4. Compromising grievance

Q. An employee was suspended for two weeks because of excessive absenteeism. At the third step of the grievance procedure, the company offered one week's back pay. Given the employee's record, we think this is a good settlement. But the employee wants us to go to arbitration to seek full back pay. If the union accepts the company's one-week offer, can the employee file a DFR charge?

A. Not successfully. A union is allowed to compromise a grievance without the grievant's approval, as long as it has good reasons and is not settling because of hostility towards the grievant.[282]

5. Backing off

Q. I filed a grievance for an employee who received a written warning for poor work. At the first-step grievance meeting, if the company presents good reasons for its actions, do I have to make a fool of myself by arguing for the employee?

A. No. Although unions must present grievances in the best possible light, they do not have to take ridiculous or impossible positions. Prior to arbitration, unions retain considerable discretion and may drop a grievance when necessary.[283]

Note: When dropping a grievance, it is good policy to give the employer a statement to the following effect: "The union does not agree with the employer's response to the grievance. Without any prejudice to its position, however, the union has decided not to process the grievance further at this time. The union reserves its right to grieve the same or similar violations in the future."[284]

6. No-smoking rule

Q. Our company has announced plans to ban smoking in work areas. 30% of our members smoke. If these employees ask the union to go to arbitration to challenge the new rule, are we obligated to do so?

A. No. Unions have a significant amount of discretion in determining whether to grieve a new work rule or job practice. Even though some members are against the new policy, the union may decide that the majority of the bargaining unit will benefit. In the absence of bad faith, a union does not breach its fair-representation duties if its decision not to grieve has a rational basis.[285]

Note: This does not mean that the union can ignore the impact of the new rule. If employees are disciplined for smoking, the union must do its best to get penalties reduced or removed.

7. Swapping grievances

Q. Two employees were suspended for leaving work early. At the third-step grievance meeting, the company offered to reinstate one employee with back pay if we drop the grievance of the second worker (who walked out early twice before). Can we accept the deal?

A. Not easily. Most unions have a policy against swapping grievances. The employee whose grievance is dropped may file a DFR charge contending that the union represented him or her less vigorously than the other employee. Nonetheless, if the union is convinced that the second employee's grievance has no chance of success, it does not violate its fair-representation duty by making a tradeoff to guarantee success for the first employee.[286]

8. Picking between employees

Q. Two employees bid for a posted job: one with nine years seniority, the other with two years. The company gave the job to the junior employee despite strong seniority provisions in our contract. We want to grieve for the senior employee, but the junior employee says if we do this, he will file DFR charges against the union. Would he have a case?

A. No. Enforcing collective-bargaining agreements often leads to conflicts between employees. The union must preserve the integrity of the contract. Carefully investigate the claims of both employees. If the company violated the contract in bypassing the senior employee, file a grievance. The union does not violate the NLRA if it makes a good-faith effort to protect the interests of the bargaining unit as a whole and is not acting out of hostility to one worker or because of a special relationship with the other.[287]

9. Steward makes mistake

Q. An employee I represent was suspended for failing to attend a company training class. I had mistakenly told her that she did not have to go to the class. Could she win a DFR case against the union because of my mistake?

A. Probably not. Poor judgment or advice, without personal hostility or bad faith, does not constitute a DFR violation.[288]

10. Employee wants grievance withdrawn

Q. Can the union keep a grievance alive if the grievant wants it withdrawn?

A. Yes, if the union feels that it is in the interests of the bargaining unit as a whole to continue the grievance.[289]

11. Considering the cost of arbitration

Q. We are grieving a four-hour overtime violation. The grievant wants us to go to arbitration, but this will probably cost the union thousands of dollars in expenses. It seems foolish to spend this much for four hour's pay — especially when the union is low on funds. Do we have to arbitrate?

A. No. Unions are allowed to consider the costs of arbitration. A union with a small treasury may not be able to arbitrate a case that a larger union could take on. The NLRA is not violated when a union, acting in good faith, declines to arbitrate for legitimate financial reasons.[290]

Note: Cost considerations carry less weight as the importance of the grievance increases. Discharge cases are the most important. Unless the case is hopeless, a union will be hard-pressed to justify a decision not to arbitrate a discharge solely because of the expense.

12. Employee agrees to pay

Q. The union's executive board voted not to take an employee's grievance to arbitration because we are afraid of losing the case and setting a precedent that will hurt other employees. The employee says she is willing to pay the arbitration fees herself and hire her own attorney. Under these circumstances, can the union refuse to take the case up?

A. Yes. The decision to arbitrate is the union's and the union's alone. Individuals cannot compel arbitration by offering to pay for it.[291]

13. Joint grievance panel

Q. The third step in our grievance procedure is a joint panel composed of two union representatives and two management representatives. Is it a DFR violation if the union's representatives vote with management to reject a union member's grievance?

A. No, unless the union representatives take their position because of personal hostility or for other discriminatory reasons.[292]

14. Business agent argues case at arbitration

Q. Does a union commit a DFR violation if a business agent handles a case at arbitration instead of the union hiring a lawyer?

A. No. A union does not violate the fair-representation duty by having a well-prepared business agent, international representative, or other union leader present the union's case at arbitration.

15. Appealing arbitration decision

Q. We lost an arbitration case for a discharged worker. The worker wants us to appeal the arbitrator's decision to federal court. The union lawyer says this would be fruitless, but the worker is threatening to sue the union. Do we have to file a court appeal?

A. No. Union grievance-processing duties extend only to contract procedures.[293] A union is not required to file a court appeal when it loses an arbitration case.

16. Statute of limitations

Q. The union dropped an employee's grievance nine months ago. Can the employee file DFR charges against the union?

A. No. The statute of limitations on DFR charges (and lawsuits) is six months. The period began the day the employee was notified that the union dropped the grievance.[294] This is a reason why union representatives should keep a record of when they inform employees that grievances are settled or dropped.

17. Suing steward

Q. If a worker files a DFR lawsuit, can she name her steward as a defendant along with the union?

A. No. DFR lawsuits may only be brought against unions. Stewards, officers, or other union representatives cannot be held personally liable.[295]

CHAPTER 8
Superseniority

MOST collective-bargaining agreements grant "superseniority" to union stewards and officers. Superseniority gives stewards and officers top seniority in their departments or job sites. The main purpose of superseniority is to prevent stewards and officers from being terminated, bumped, or transferred during layoffs. A laid-off steward cannot properly investigate grievances or provide other necessary services.

Prior to 1975, unions were free to negotiate superseniority provisions. However, in *Dairylea Cooperative,*

Inc., the NLRB imposed restrictions, contending that many superseniority clauses provided more protection than was necessary to guarantee representation and constituted unlawful union favoritism.[296]

The NLRB was especially concerned about clauses giving superseniority to executive-board members, trustees, and other union officials who, in some workplaces, do not take part in grievance processing or contract administration.

Who Can Use Superseniority?

Under the *Dairylea* decision, superseniority may be utilized only by union representatives who engage in *day-to-day grievance processing* or who have other *regular on-the-job contract administration responsibilities*. Union stewards almost always fall within these requirements. Officers, executive-board members, and other union officials may use superseniority if their on-the-job presence is necessary to ensure effective employee representation.[297]

Note: The duties of union officials, not their titles, determine whether superseniority may be utilized. For example, in many unions, executive-board members take an active part in grievance processing and can therefore take advantage of superseniority provisions.

How Much Protection?

Superseniority clauses may not provide unnecessary benefits. Clauses which protect against layoffs, grant preferences for recall, or prevent stewards from being bumped are legal. But, clauses which favor stewards for better job assignments, choice of vacations, or selection of days off violate the NLRA.[298]

Pay For Stewards?

Section 302 of the NLRA makes it illegal for employers to pay union representatives except "as compensation for their services as employees." This law has led some employers to claim that they must dock the wages of stewards and union officers for time spent on union business despite contract provisions or past practices calling for full wages. These employers are wrong. As long as a steward (or other union representative) spends time each day or week as an *active working employee*, it is lawful for an employer to compensate the employee for union-business time — even if the union time is several hours per day.[299]

Section 302 may be violated if employers continue wages for employees who become *full-time* union officials.[300] But it is not illegal to permit such officials to accrue pension credits or receive other fringe benefits negotiated in a collective-bargaining agreement.[301]

QUESTIONS AND ANSWERS

1. Overtime preference

Q. Our superseniority clause gives stewards preferences for overtime assignments. Is this legal?

A. Yes, but use of the clause must be restricted to periods when more than one employee is needed.[302]

2. Departmental protection

Q. Can a superseniority clause be used to prevent a steward from being bumped to a different department during a layoff?

A. Yes. If stewards are selected by departments, a super-seniority clause can be used to prevent a steward from being bumped from his or her area of representation.[303]

3. Shift protection

Q. Can a superseniority clause be used to prevent a steward from being bumped to a different shift?

A. Yes — if the steward is selected by employees on a particular shift and is responsible to these employees.[304]

4. Recording secretary

Q. Can a superseniority clause be used by a recording secretary?

A. Probably not. Recording secretaries usually do not have an active role in the grievance process.[305]

5. Union president

Q. Can a union president use superseniority?

A. Yes. Union presidents usually play an important role in contract administration, often meeting with management on problems before they become formal grievances.[306]

6. High ratio

Q. Our company is reducing operations. If we follow the superseniority clause, we will be left with six stewards and four officers out of a workforce of 35. Any problems?

A. Perhaps. Although the NLRB says it is the role of union personnel, not the ratio of representatives to employees, that determines whether superseniority can be applied,[307] the small number of employees may make it difficult for the union to prove a need for 10 representatives. Stewards, unlike officers, enjoy a presumption of necessity and are more likely to survive a legal challenge at the NLRB.

7. Higher pay for stewards?

Q. Can the union negotiate a contract clause awarding higher hourly wages for stewards?

A. No. Such a clause gives a monetary benefit exclusively to stewards without being necessary to guarantee effective representation.[308]

Note: The NLRA does not prevent a union from paying officers or stewards from the union treasury.

8. Contract expiration

Q. What will happen to superseniority if our contract expires?

A. It continues as a binding term of employment unless the employer demands its elimination and bargains its demand to the point of impasse.[309]

CHAPTER 9
Choosing Union Stewards

OW STEWARDS are chosen is determined by union bylaws and constitutional provisions. These provisions can be enforced as contracts by union members. The NLRA prohibits employers from attempting to influence the selection of stewards. Another federal law, the Labor-Management Reporting and Disclosure Act (LMRDA, popularly known as the Landrum-Griffin Act),[310] also has a bearing on choosing stewards.

Must Stewards Be Elected?

One question commonly asked is whether stewards must be elected by the employees they represent. The answer, according to the nation's labor laws, is no. Although the Landrum-Griffin Act requires "constitutional officers" to be elected, stewards are not officers. Under most union bylaws, stewards are elected by a department or shift. But in a great many unions, stewards are appointed by the union president or business agent. Appointing stewards is lawful.

Qualifications

Qualifications for stewards are usually set out in the union's bylaws or constitution. The only restrictions imposed by federal law concern persons who have been convicted of serious crimes.

Section 504(a) of the Landrum-Griffin Act bars persons convicted of certain crimes from holding union positions. The bar applies to officers, trustees, agents, executive-board members, employees, and any other person "who serves as a representative in any capacity of any labor organization."[311]

Listed crimes. The Section 504(a) disqualification applies to the following offenses: robbery, bribery, extortion, embezzlement, grand larceny, burglary, arson, violation of narcotics laws, murder, rape, assault with intent to kill, assault which inflicts grievous bodily injury, violation of LMRDA reporting or trusteeship requirements, felonious abuse of union position or employee benefit plan, or conspiracy or attempt to commit such crimes.

Note: Under federal law when Section 504(a) was adopted, the term narcotic was defined as "opium, coca leaves, and opiates" or preparations which are derived from or chemically identical to these substances.[312] Marijuana does not fall within this definition, nor do depressant or stimulant substances.

Duration. The bar from union office lasts 13 years from date of conviction or from date of release from prison, whichever is later. Individuals can ask the sentencing judge to shorten the period (to no less than three years). They can also petition a federal court to exempt them from the bar. Failure to adhere to the disqualification can result in fines against individuals and the union of up to $10,000 and imprisonment for up to five years.

Removal From Office

Unions can remove stewards from office (subject to procedures in the union's bylaws or constitution) if stewards fail to perform their duties or take part in wrongdoing. The ability to remove stewards for political reasons, however, depends on whether the steward is appointed or elected.

In 1982, the U.S. Supreme Court gave unions the right to remove *appointed officials* for political reasons. In *Finnegan v. Leu,* the Court declared:

> The ability of an elected union president to select his own administrators is an integral part of ensuring a union administration's responsiveness to the mandate of the union election.[313]

The Court noted, however, that if the purpose of the dismissals was to suppress dissent within the union, it would violate Section 401 of the Landrum-Griffith Act, which protects union members' free speech.

Elected union officials, including stewards, have a much stronger legal position. A 1991 Supreme Court decision ruled that the removal of elected officials, solely for political reasons, violates the Landrum-Griffin Act.[314]

QUESTIONS AND ANSWERS

1. Election procedures

Q. If a union elects stewards, must it follow the rules regarding nominations, secret ballots, and voting found in the Landrum-Griffin Act?

A. No. Landrum-Griffin rules apply only to elections of constitutional officers.[315] Because stewards are not officers, the only election procedures that must be adhered to are those in the union's bylaws or constitution.

2. Criminal conviction

Q. I was convicted of cocaine possession in 1983 and spent six months in jail. Can I run for union office in 1994?

A. Yes. The 13-year bar on holding union office applies only to convictions after October 12, 1984.

3. Bonding

Q. Must union stewards be bonded?

A. No. Under federal law, bonding is required only for union officials who handle funds or other union property.[316]

4. Construction union steward

Q. Our union has a hiring hall arrangement under which we refer carpenters to contractors based on their rank on an out-of-work list. Can we deviate from the list in order to refer a particular employee to be the steward for a job?

A. Yes. The NLRB recognizes the right of a union to select, in good faith, whomever it considers to be the best choice to serve as steward — even if this requires deviating from the normal order of a referral list.[317]

5. Refusal to hire steward

Q. Can an employer refuse to hire an individual referred by a union because he or she has been designated as the union steward?

A. No. Refusing to accept an individual for employment because he or she has been designated a union steward is an unfair labor practice.[318]

6. Conditioning reinstatement on resignation from steward post

Q. A steward was discharged for drinking at lunch, returning to work late, and threatening a foreman. At the grievance hearing, the company said the steward could return to work, but as an employee only and not as a steward. Isn't this illegal?

A. Probably, yes. The NLRB long held that an employer violates the NLRA by conditioning an employee's reinstatement on his or her agreeing not to hold union office.[319] In 1992, however, the Board relaxed its rule by sanctioning a "last chance agreement" with five employees who took part in a mid-contract strike.[320] The Board said that because the five had shown "contempt" for the collective-bargaining agreement, the employer could seek an agreement in which the employees relinquished their rights to hold union office. The steward's conduct in your case, however, does not appear to rise to the level of "contempt" that would allow an employer to insist on giving up union-office rights.

7. Employer influences election

Q. A supervisor is advising employees to vote for a certain candidate because, "I need a steward I can talk to." Is this allowed?

A. No. It is an unfair labor practice for an employer to attempt to influence the results of a union election.[321]

CHAPTER 10

Other Labor Laws that Stewards Can Use

T HERE ARE many important labor laws besides the NLRA. This chapter discusses federal laws. Request descriptions of state laws from the labor agencies in your state.

Fair Labor Standards Act

The Fair Labor Standards Act (known as FLSA) was passed by Congress in 1938.[322] It establishes the minimum wage level (currently $4.25 per hour), sets child labor standards, and mandates overtime wages. The FLSA covers most employers and employees, although there are numerous exemptions, including railroad, air carrier, and trucking employees. State and local government employees are covered by the FLSA. The law is enforced by the U.S. Department of Labor Wage and Hour Division and by private lawsuit.

Because the FLSA overtime requirement of one and one-half pay is duplicated in almost all collective-bargaining agreements, unions usually file contract grievances over overtime issues, rather than utilizing the slower procedures of the Wage and Hour Division. Nevertheless, there are times when the FLSA comes in handy.

• **Definitions of work time.** FLSA regulations provide definitions of "hours worked." The regulations should be consulted when there is a dispute about whether employees are entitled to receive pay for such periods as: waiting time, rest periods, meal periods, changing-clothes time, travel time, on-call time, grievance time, or work-at-home time. Ask the Wage and Hour Division local office for a copy of their publication, *Hours Worked Under the Fair Labor Standards Act of 1938.*

- **Two jobs worked.** When employees are assigned to lower-paid jobs on overtime, should they receive one and one-half: (1) their usual hourly rate; (2) the rate on the second job; or (3) a weighted average of the two jobs? FLSA regulations mandate blended rates — unless the union agrees otherwise.[323]

- **Non-scheduled overtime.** Some employees put in extra time without realizing they are entitled to over-time pay. For example, they may have a habit of beginning work early, working through their meal breaks, working after their shift ends, or working at home. Under the FLSA, employers must pay an over-time premium for work they *assign, permit, have knowledge of, or should have knowledge of.*[324] Over-time work does not have to be requested, scheduled, or be on the clock. Employees can put in claims for up to three years of back wages when they learn of their rights.

Family and Medical Leave Act

The Family and Medical Leave Act (known as the FMLA) was passed in 1993.[325] It covers private-sector employers with 50 or more employees and all state and local governmental agencies. It is enforced by the U.S. Department of Labor Wage and Hour Division.

The FMLA guarantees employees up to 12 weeks of unpaid leave each year to:
1. Care for an immediate family member (spouse, child, or parent) with a serious health condition
2. Care for a newborn child, newly adopted child, or newly placed foster child
3. Treat or recover from a serious health condition (a term which includes long-term and chronic conditions as well as injuries, illnesses, and mental conditions causing incapacities of more than three consecutive calendar days with continuing treatment by a health care provider).

The FMLA supersedes contract provisions which provide for less than 12 weeks time off. Leave requests for FMLA purposes must be granted — including the allowance of part-time or reduced-week schedules for employees with serious health conditions. Employers cannot impose penalties for FMLA absences and must return employees to their jobs (or equivalent positions). Group health insurance benefits must be continued during the leave.

To be entitled to an FMLA leave, employees must satisfy three eligibility tests:
1. They must have worked for the employer for a total of at least 12 months (consecutive or non-consecutive).
2. They must have worked at least 1,250 hours for the employer during the previous 12 months.
3. They must work at a location where at least 50 employees are employed by the employer within 75 miles.

The FMLA gives unions a tool to defend employees who face discipline or discharge for health-related attendance problems. For example, an employee under treatment for a chronic back condition must be allowed up to 60 days off per year (12 work weeks) without penalty. This makes it difficult, if not impossible, for employers to enforce so-called "no fault" absenteeism policies.

Literature about the FMLA can be obtained from your local Wage and Hour Division office. You should file complaints with this office if employees are denied an FMLA leave, are not given their jobs back, or are punished for absences covered by the FMLA.

Occupational Safety and Health Act

The Occupational Safety and Health Act (known as the OSH Act) was passed by Congress in 1970.[326]

The OSH Act is enforced by the Occupational Safety and Health Administration (known as OSHA). In some states, the OSH Act is enforced by state agencies.

OSHA has jurisdiction over private-sector employers, regardless of size, except for industries that are regulated by other federal agencies, such as mining, railroads, nuclear power, and trucking. The OSH Act establishes health and safety standards for various jobs and industries. OSHA inspectors make unannounced visits to workplaces according to their own schedules and in response to complaints from individuals and unions.

OSHA can fine enterprises up to $70,000 for willful or repeat violations and up to $7,000 for each other violation. OSHA can order employers to close down dangerous machinery or work areas.

An OSHA regulation allows an employee to refuse unsafe work if the following conditions exist:
1. The employee has a reasonable belief, based on what he or she knows at the time, that there is a real danger of death or serious physical injury.

2. The employee asks the employer to eliminate the danger, but the employer fails to do so.
3. The danger is so urgent that the employee cannot risk waiting until OSHA can conduct an inspection.
4. The employee has no reasonable alternative.[327]

The U.S. Department of Transportation has a similar rule for employees in the trucking industry.[328]

(The NLRA also has a provision allowing employees, in certain situations, to refuse unsafe work. The work must be "abnormally dangerous."[329])

Stewards can use the OSH Act in many ways:

- They can obtain copies of OSHA standards and study the rules that apply to their work-place.
- They can report violations of standards by filing an OSHA com-plaint, or, in an emergency, calling the agency for an immedi-ate inspec-tion. OSHA does not reveal the names of com-plainants.
- They can inform employees who are disciplined for refus-ing unsafe work of their right to file an OSHA complaint. It is illegal for employers to take reprisals against

employees who file OSHA complaints or provide OSHA with information.

Title VII

Title VII is part of the 1964 Federal Civil Rights Act.[330] It forbids employment discrimination on the basis of race, color, sex, national origin, or religion.

Title VII applies to private-sector employers with more than 15 employees and to state and local government employers. It is enforced by the Equal Employment Opportunity Commission (the EEOC). Employees may also sue in court.

Title VII violations can be expensive for employers. In addition to lost pay and benefits, Title VII allows victims of intentional discrimination to sue for *punitive damages*.

Title VII is violated if:

- Employers favor one racial group or one gender group in hiring, promotions, job assignments, or the enforcement of work rules.
- Employers establish criteria for hiring, promotions, or transfers, such as experience requirements or high school diplomas, which tend to screen out women or minorities without a business necessity for the requirement.
- Employers or supervisors harass employees in a sexual manner, or because of their race, or tolerate harassment by employees, customers, or contractors.

Employees who are discriminated against or are harassed can file charges at the EEOC or at state anti-discrimination agencies. Stewards should help employees to contact these agencies.

Americans with Disabilities Act

The Americans with Disabilities Act (known as the ADA) was passed by Congress in 1990.[331] It forbids discrimination against qualified persons with disabilities and requires employers to make *reasonable accommodations* to the restrictions and limitations of disabled job applicants and employees.

The ADA covers private- and public-sector employers with 15 or more employees. It is enforced by the Equal Employment Opportunity Commission (the EEOC). Employees may also sue in court.

The ADA has clout. Employers that discriminate, or refuse to provide accommodations, can be assessed substantial damages.

Stewards can use ADA charges, or threats to file charges, in many ways:

- To force an employer to purchase special machinery so that an employee with a disability can perform his or her job
- To make an employer reassign job duties so that a disabled employee can stay on the job or get a promotion
- To enable a disabled employee to obtain a leave of absence greater than the 12 weeks provided by the FMLA
- To force an employer to respect the lifting or other medical restrictions applicable to a disabled employee

Employers do not have to make accommodations if the changes needed by the employee would create an "undue hardship" for the employer's business or if, even with accommodations, the employee cannot perform the essential duties of the position.

Employees who are discriminated against or whose requests for accommodation are denied should file complaints at the nearest EEOC office.

Other Laws

- **Age Discrimination in Employment Act (ADEA).**[332] Prohibits discrimination on the basis of age against employees or job applicants 40 years old or older. Forbids mandatory retirement at any age over 40 (with a few exceptions). Enforced by the Equal Employment Opportunity Commission (EEOC) and by private lawsuit.
- **Davis-Bacon Act.**[333] Requires prevailing wages for workers on federally financed construction work. Enforced by the U.S. Department of Labor Wage and Hour Division.
- **Employee Polygraph Protection Act.**[334] Prohibits most private-sector employers from using lie detector tests either for pre-employment screening or during the course of employment. Exceptions apply to security firms, drug companies, and to employees suspected of theft. Enforced by the U.S. Department of Labor and by private lawsuit.
- **Employee Retirement Income Security Act (ERISA).**[335] Regulates pension, health, and welfare plans. Establishes vesting rights. Protects employees in the event of bankruptcies. Mandates prudent investment of pension assets. Enforced by the U.S. Department of Labor and by private lawsuit.
- **Equal Pay Act (EPA).**[336] Requires that men and woman be paid equal wages for work of equal character in the same establishment. Enforced by the Equal Employment Opportunity Commission (EEOC) and by private lawsuit.

- **Executive Order 11246.** Prohibits discrimination based on race, religion, sex, or national origin by employers who do at least $10,000 worth of business per year with the federal government. Affirmative action is required of federal contractors with contracts over $50,000. Contractors may be debarred for violations. Enforced by the Office of Federal Contract Compliance Programs (OFCCP).

- **Immigration and Nationality Act.**[337] Forbids employers from hiring unauthorized alien workers. Requires new employees to fill out government biographical forms. Makes it illegal to restrict hiring to U.S. citizens except when citizenship is required by law or government contract. Enforced by the EEOC, the U.S. Department of Justice, and by private lawsuit.

- **Labor-Management Reporting and Disclosure Act (LMRDA).**[338] Regulates private-sector unions. Establishes union members' "bill of rights." Requires fair elections. Establishes rules for disciplinary procedures. Sets out standards for trusteeships. Enforced by the U.S. Department of Labor Office of Labor-Management Standards and by private lawsuit.

- **Walsh-Healey Act.**[339] Establishes minimum wage and overtime pay standards for workers engaged in the manufacture or furnishing of materials to federal agencies under a contract exceeding $10,000. Enforced by the U.S. Department of Labor Wage and Hour Division.

- **Worker Adjustment and Retraining Notification Act (WARN).**[340] Requires covered employers (100 or more employees) to provide 60 days advance notice of plant closings and mass layoffs. Employees may sue for lost wages in U.S. district court.

GLOSSARY

ALJ: Abbreviation for administrative law judge. ALJs conduct unfair-labor-practice hearings for the National Labor Relations Board.

Arbitration: A method of settling grievance disputes. A person called an arbitrator is chosen and given the power to make a binding decision.

Collective-bargaining agreement: The contract between the employer and the union, usually written, fixing conditions of employment for a period of time.

Concerted activity: Actions taken by two or more employees for mutual aid or protection. Actions by one employee are included if the employee is seeking to benefit other employees or is seeking to enforce the collective-bargaining agreement. Activities must be concerted to come within the protection of Section 7 of the NLRA.

Confidentiality agreement: An agreement in which the employer consents to supply the union with confidential information and the union agrees not to reveal the information.

Deferral: A policy of the NLRB not to process unfair-labor-practice charges if the charge can be filed as a grievance and taken up through a grievance and arbitration procedure. The NLRB reviews the resulting grievance settlement or arbitration decision. If it is "clearly repugnant" to the NLRA, the NLRB issues a complaint.

Duty of fair representation (DFR): The duty of a union to represent all employees in the bargaining unit without discrimination, hostility, or personal bias. Unions that commit DFR violations can be charged with unfair labor practices at the NLRB or sued in court.

Grievant: An employee who files a grievance or an employee for whom the union files a grievance.

Impasse: The point in bargaining where there is no prospect of change of position by either party. When impasse is reached, the employer is free to implement changes consistent with its last bargaining position.

Mandatory bargaining subject: A subject pertaining to wages, hours, terms, or conditions of employment. An employer may not make a change in a mandatory bargaining subject without providing prior notice to the union and an opportunity to bargain.

Management-rights clause: A provision found in most collective-bargaining agreements delegating certain rights to management, generally including the right to direct the enterprise, assign work, and sometimes including the right to establish disciplinary or work rules. The wording in a management-rights clause is important in determining whether a union has waived any of its bargaining rights during the term of the contract.

The National Labor Relations Act (NLRA): Federal law passed in 1935 giving employees the right to join unions, bargain collectively, and strike. Also known as the Taft-Hartley Act and the Labor Management Relations Act (LMRA).

The National Labor Relations Board (NLRB): Federal agency that enforces the NLRA.

No-strike clause: A provision found in most collective-bargaining agreements in which the union pledges that there will be no strikes during the term of the agreement. The wording of the no-strike clause determines whether union officials, including stewards, can be held to higher responsibilities for taking part in contract-barred work stoppages.

Past practice: A customary way of doing things not written into the collective-bargaining agreement. Past practices can sometimes be enforced through the grievance procedure if the practice has been longstanding, consistent, and accepted by the parties. Past-practice grievances concerning employee benefits are more successful than past-practice grievances concerning methods of operation.

Preliminary injunction: An order by a federal or state judge restoring the status quo pending litigation. The NLRB can request preliminary injunctions in unfair-labor-practice cases.

Section 7 rights: Activities protected by Section 7 of the NLRA such as union organizing, grievance processing, picketing, and strikes. Employers may not interfere with, threaten, or discriminate against employees for taking part in Section 7 activities.

Statute of limitations: The period during which a complaint must be filed under a state or federal law. Under the NLRA, Title VII, and most federal labor laws, the statute of limitations is six months from the date notice is given of an adverse action.

Superseniority: A benefit provided by many union contracts to stewards and other union officials. Superseniority usually places stewards and officers at the top of the seniority ladder to protect them in the case of layoffs.

Unfair labor practice: A violation of the NLRA by the employer or the union.

Unilateral change: A change in a mandatory bargaining subject made by an employer without prior notice and/or bargaining. Unless permitted by the contract, unilateral changes are unfair labor practices.

Voluntary bargaining subject (same as permissive bargaining subject): A subject about which the employer can legally refuse to bargain; for example, the selection of management personnel.

Waiver: An intentional giving up of a right provided by the NLRA such as the right to bargain over mid-term changes. To qualify as a waiver, a contract clause must "clearly and unmistakably" give up NLRA rights.

Weingarten rights: The rights of employees to request union representation during investigatory interviews and the rights of union representatives to assist and counsel employees during interviews.

FOOTNOTES

THE CITATIONS in the footnotes refer mainly to NLRB and court decisions. The volumes containing these decisions are called "reporters." They can usually be found in courthouse, law school, and large public libraries.

NLRB decisions. Decisions of the NLRB are published in a reporter called *Decisions and Orders of the National Labor Relations Board*, abbreviated as NLRB. Volume numbers come first, followed by page numbers.

NLRB decisions also appear in digest form in a reporter called the *Labor Relations Reference Manual* (LRRM). The LRRM citation appears after the NLRB citation. (LRRM volumes always begin at page 1001).

Court decisions. Federal court decisions appear in reporters with the following abbreviations:

F. Supp.   Federal Supplement (decisions of the United States District Courts)

F.2d   Federal Reporter Second Series (decisions of the United States Circuit Courts)

U.S.   Decisions of the United States Supreme Court.

Circuit court decisions are often preceded by the words *enforced, enforced as modified*, or *enforcement denied*, depending on how the circuit court ruled on the appeal from the underlying NLRB decision.

Other Abbreviations:

LA   Labor Arbitration Reports

U.S.C.   United States Code

CFR   Code of Federal Regulations

Example: Indiana & Michigan Electric Co., 273 NLRB 654, 118 LRRM 1177 (1985), *enforced*, 786 F.2d 733,

121 LRRM 3259 (6th Cir. 1986) means the NLRB decision is found in volume 273 of the NLRB reporter,
beginning at page 654. The decision is also found (in
digest form) in volume 118 of the LRRM, beginning at
page 1177. The decision was issued in 1985. The citation indicates that the NLRB decision was enforced by a
Sixth Circuit decision in 1986. The court decision can
be found in volume 786 of the Federal Reporter Second
Series, beginning at page 733. The court case is also
found (in full) in volume 121 of the LRRM, beginning
at page 3259.

Ordering cases
from Work Rights Press

You can order NLRB decisions from Work Rights Press.
See page 181 for an order blank.

1. The NLRA is codified as 29 U.S.C. §141 *et seq.* It is
   sometimes referred to as the Wagner Act, the Labor
   Management Relations Act (LMRA), and the Taft-
   Hartley Act. **Note:** Although section numbers in the Act
   go into the 500s, there are many gaps: the actual number
   of sections is 42.

2. Union unfair labor practices also include restraint of
   employees (8(b)(1)(A)); causing employer to discriminate against employees (8(b)(2)); refusing to bargain in
   good faith (8(b)(3)); engaging in secondary strikes, boycotts, or picketing (8(b)(4)); and engaging in recogni-
   tional picketing for longer than thirty days (8(b)(7)).

3. *See* Country Cubbard Corp., 179 NLRB 53, 72 LRRM
   1255 (1969) (dismissal even though employer threatened
   to discipline employees for bringing grievances to
   union's attention); *but see* General Motors Corp., 232
   NLRB 335, 97 LRRM 1162 (1977)(single threat against
   employee for using grievance system sufficient to war-

rant violation); Container Corporation of America, 244 NLRB 318, 102 LRRM 1162 (1979) (threat by plant manager to make it "hard" on union officer, not isolated or de minimis).

4. Collyer Insulated Wire, 192 NLRB 837, 77 LRRM 1931 (1971).

5. Olin Corp. 268 NLRB 573, 115 LRRM 1056 (1984). *See* Spielberg Mfg. Co., 112 NLRB 1080, 36 LRRM 1152 (1955).

6. *See,* e.g., Joseph T. Ryerson and Sons, Inc., 199 NLRB 461, 81 LRRM 1261 (1972); North Shore Publishing Co., 206 NLRB 42, 84 LRRM 1165 (1973); Clara Barton Terrace Convalescent Center, 225 NLRB 1028, 92 LRRM 1621 (1976).

7. United Technologies Corp., 268 NLRB 557, 115 LRRM 1049 (1984).

8. U.S. Postal Service, 280 NLRB 685, 122 LRRM 1337 (1986).

9. Grand Rapids Die Casting Corp., 279 NLRB 662, 122 LRRM 1212 (1986).

10. Southwestern Bell Telephone Co., 276 NLRB 1053, 120 LRRM 1145 (1985).

11. When an arbitration is held on a dispute deferred by the NLRB, consider using an attorney, selecting an arbitrator with a knowledge of labor law, arranging for a stenographic record, and submitting a legal brief.

12. *See*, *e.g.*, Cone Mills Corp., 298 NLRB 661, 134 LRRM 1105 (1990); Garland Coal & Mining Co., 276 NLRB 963, 120 LRRM 1159 (1985); Union Fork & Hoe Co., 241 NLRB 907, 101 LRRM 1014 (1979).

13. *See* 29 CFR 102.118(b)(1). Employer requests under the Freedom of Information Act (FOIA) for employee affidavits in closed cases are generally refused by the NLRB based on exemptions 7(A), 7(C), and 7(D) of the FOIA.

14. Preliminary relief is available under 29 U.S.C. §160(j).

15. *See* Tiidee Products, Inc., 196 NLRB 158, 79 LRRM 1692 (1972), *enforced*, 502 F.2d 349, 86 LRRM 2093 (D.C. Cir. 1974).

16. Cone Mills Corp. 298 NLRB 661, 134 LRRM 1105 (1990).

17. *See* Pennsylvania Energy Corp., 274 NLRB 1153, 119 LRRM 1042 (1985).

18. 45 U.S.C. §§151-163.

19. 5 U.S.C. §7101 *et. seq.*

20. Hawaiian Hauling Service, Ltd., 219 NLRB 765, 766 n. 6, 90 LRRM 1011, 1013 n.6 (1975) (emphasis supplied).

21. Letter Carriers v. Austin, 418 U.S. 264, 283, 86 LRRM 2740, 2476 (U.S. Sup. Ct. 1974). *Accord*, Severance Tool Industries, 301 NLRB 1166, 1170, 137 LRRM 1045 (1991) (certain amount of "salty language and defiance" must be tolerated during grievance meeting).

22. The Bettcher Mfg, Corp., 76 NLRB 526, 527, 21 LRRM 1222, 1223 (1948). *See, e.g.*, Calmos Combining Co., 184 NLRB 914, 74 LRRM 1693 (1970) (loud disruptive conversation on shop floor); Charles Myers & Co., 190 NLRB 448, 77 LRRM 1304 (1971) (telling supervisor he "should have his mouth bashed in").

23. U.S. Postal Service, 256 NLRB 736, 107 LRRM 1336 (1981).

24. Boespflug Construction Co., 113 NLRB 330, 36 LRRM 1296 (1955).

25. Clara Barton Terrace Convalescent Center, 225 NLRB 1028, 92 LRRM 1621 (1976).

26. Metropolitan Life Insurance Co., 258 NLRB 61, 108 LRRM 1282 (1981).

27. *See* Bell Halter, Inc., 276 NLRB 1208, 120 LRRM 1322 (1985).

28. Metropolitan Life Ins. Co., 258 NLRB 61, 108 LRRM 1282 (1981).

29. *Id.*

30. Great Falls White Truck Co., 183 NLRB 539, 74 LRRM 1510 (1970).

31. Caterpillar Tractor Co., 242 NLRB 523, 101 LRRM 1207 (1979).

32. Beverly California Corp., 310 NLRB 222, 142 LRRM 1169 (1993); U.S. Postal Service, 266 NLRB 467, 112 LRRM 1429 (1983). Threatening a union staff member, such as a business agent, in front of employees, is also a violation. Beverly California Corp., *supra.*

33. Metropolitan Life Insurance Co., 258 NLRB 61, 108 LRRM 1282 (1981).

34. Studio 44, Inc., 284 NLRB 597, 125 LRRM 1203 (1987).

35. Advance Window Corp., 291 NLRB 226, 130 LRRM 1080 (1988).

36. *See, e.g.*, Union Fork & Hoe Co., 241 NLRB 907, 101 LRRM 1014 (1979); Owens Corning Fiberglas Co., 236 NLRB 479, 98 LRRM 1234 (1978). **Note:** Unfortunately, some arbitrators, probably unfamiliar with the NLRA, continue to take the mistaken position that stewards are supposed to set examples in terms of work and conduct. This is a strong reason why unions should file NLRB charges whenever stewards are wrongly disciplined.

37. Indiana & Michigan Electric Co., 273 NLRB 654, 118 LRRM 1177 (1985), *enforced*, 786 F.2d 733, 121 LRRM 3259 (6th Cir. 1986).

38. Midwest Precision Castings Co., 244 NLRB 597, 102 LRRM 1074 (1979); *but see* Eagle Picher Industries, 278 NLRB 696, 121 LRRM 1253 (1986) (discharge of grievance committeeman for presence on picket line, violation).

39. Clarkson Industries, 312 NLRB No. 63, 144 LRRM 1215 (1993).

40. Synadyne Corp., 228 NLRB 664, 96 LRRM 1587 (1977).

41. American Telephone and Telegraph Co., 211 NLRB 782, 86 LRRM 1645 (1974).

42. Hawaiian Hauling Service, Ltd., 219 NLRB 765, 90 LRRM 1011 (1975). **Note:** The equality rule is sometimes applied to rank-and-file employees who take part in grievance meetings. *See* Crown Central Petroleum Corp., 430 F.2d 724, 74 LRRM 2855. (5th Cir. 1970).

43. Max Factor & Co., 239 NLRB 804, 100 LRRM 1023 (1978).

44. U.S. Postal Service, 250 NLRB 4, 104 LRRM 1300 (1980).

45. Consumers Power Co., 245 NLRB 183, 102 LRRM 1500 (1979). Calling a foreman a "f-----g incompetent asshole" was deemed protected by an ALJ in United Technologies Corp., 274 NLRB 504, 512-513, 118 LRRM 1464 (1985) (Board voted to defer the 8(a)(1) charges). Calling company president a "son of a bitch" was protected in Severance Tool Industries, 301 NLRB 1166, 137 LRRM 1045 (1991).

46. U.S. Postal Service, 251 NLRB 252, 105 LRRM 1033, 1034 (1980), *enforced*, 652 F.2d 409, 107 LRRM 3249 (5th Cir. 1981).

47. Container Corp. of America, 255 NLRB 1404, 107 LRRM 1126 (1981).

48. Ryder Truck Lines, Inc., 239 NLRB 1009, 100 LRRM 1097 (1978). *See also* BASF Wyandotte Corp., 278 NLRB 225, 122 LRRM 1152 (1986) (tearing up company rule and throwing it in wastebasket during grievance meeting, protected).

49. Charles Myers & Co., 190 NLRB 448, 77 LRRM 1304 (1971). *See also* Calmos Combining Co., 184 NLRB

914, 74 LRRM 1693 (1970) (shouting on the shop floor); Chrysler Corp., 249 NLRB 1102, 104 LRRM 1314 (1980) (steward pursued supervisor relentlessly, engaged in loud abusive conduct, and threatened to continue the conduct for the entire shift); U.S. Postal Service, 268 NLRB 274, 114 LRRM 1281 (1983) (refusing order to quiet down, causing disruption of operations).

50. Cone Mills Corp., 273 NLRB 1515, 134 LRRM 1105 (1990).

51. U.S. Postal Service, 250 NLRB 1195, 105 LRRM 1014 (1980).

52. *See, e.g.*, Hasten v. Phillips Petroleum Co., 640 F.2d 274, 106 LRRM 2547 (10th Cir. 1981); Gregory v. Simon Bros., 640 F. Supp. 1252, 123 LRRM 2424 (N.D Ind. 1986). **Note:** The supervisor's threat to sue is an unfair labor practice. Consolidated Edison Co. of New York, 286 NLRB 1031, 126 LRRM 1305 (1987) (threat by manager "to sue your ass off").

53. *See* Tosti v. Ayik, 437 N.E.2d 1062, 114 LRRM 2558 (Mass. 1982).

54. Square D Co., 204 NLRB 154, 83 LRRM 1293 (1973). Section 8(c) of the NLRA permits employers to express views, arguments, or opinions concerning unions if the expressions contain no threats of reprisal or force. NLRB v. Raytheon Co., 445 F.2d 272, 77 LRRM 2726 (9th Cir. 1971).

55. Lenkurt Electronic Co., Inc., 182 NLRB 510, 74 LRRM 1182 (1970), *enforced*, 459 F.2d 635, 80 LRRM 635 (9th Cir. 1972).

56. U.S. Postal Service, 256 NLRB 736, 107 LRRM 1336 (1981).

57. Studio 44, Inc., 284 NLRB 597, 125 LRRM 1203 (1987).

58. Metropolitan Life Ins. Co., 258 NLRB 61, 108 LRRM 1282 (1981); Wald Mfg. Co., 176 NLRB 839, 73 LRRM 1486 (1969).

59. *See* Asphalt Paving Co., 224 NLRB 265, 92 LRRM 1368 (1976).

60. Markle Mfg. Co., 239 NLRB 1353, 100 LRRM 1230 (1979); Cooper-Jarrett, Inc., 260 NLRB 1123, 109 LRRM 1265 (1982) (foreman tells steward, "I wish you didn't work for this company," violation).

61. Caterpillar Tractor Co., 242 NLRB 523, 101 LRRM 1207 (1979).

62. Owens Corning Fiberglas Co., 236 NLRB 479, 98 LRRM 1234 (1978). *See* Metropolitan Edison Co. v. NLRB, 460 U.S. 698, 112 LRRM 3265 (U.S. Sup. Ct. 1983).

63. Outboard Marine Corp., 253 NLRB 486, 105 LRRM 1674 (1980). *See also* Consolidated Freightways Corp. of Delaware, 257 NLRB 1281, 108 LRRM 1165 (1981) (illegal to threaten steward for bypassing chain of command by meeting with higher management officials).

64. Cook Paint & Varnish Co., 258 NLRB 1230, n. 9, 108 LRRM 1150, n. 9 (1981).

65. *See* Alton Box Board Co., 155 NLRB 1025, 60 LRRM 1458 (1965); Levingston Shipbuilding Co., 249 NLRB 81, 104 LRRM 1058 (1980); IUE Local 320, 117 LRRM 1510 (Advice Memorandum 1984).

66. *See* Manville Forest Products Corp., 269 NLRB 390, 115 LRRM 1266 (1984); Cook Paint & Varnish Co., 246 NLRB 646, 102 LRRM 1680 (1979). *See also* Service Technology Corp., 196 NLRB 845, 80 LRRM 1187 (1972) (employee has no right to refuse to answer questions about misconduct he has been involved in or has witnessed).

67. Ford Motor Co., 3 LA 779 (Shulman, Arbitrator).

68. NLRB v. City Disposal Systems, 465 U.S. 822, 115 LRRM 3193 (U.S. Sup. Ct. 1984). *Accord* Michigan Screw Products, 242 NLRB 811, 101 LRRM 1277 (1979) (refusal to work overtime). *See* ABF Fleet Systems, Inc., 271

NLRB 35, 116 LRRM 1330 (1984) (refusal to drive truck with defective brakes).

69. Carolina Freight Carriers Corp. 295 NLRB 1080, 131 LRRM 1762 (1989).

70. Entenman's Bakery, 77 LA 1081 (Ness, Arbitrator).

71. General Motors Corp., 233 NLRB 47, 96 LRRM 1398 (1977).

72. *See* Rockwell International, 278 NLRB 55, 122 LRRM 1285 (1986), *enforced*, 814 F.2d 1530, 125 LRRM 2132 (11th Cir. 1987).

73. Pacific Coast Utilities Service, Inc., 238 NLRB 599, 99 LRRM 161 (1978), *enforced*, 638 F.2d 73, 104 LRRM 2320 (9th Cir. 1980). **Note:** In two later cases the NLRB withheld protection from employees who refused to sign warning slips. But these cases involved nonunion employees whose actions were not related to union or other collective activity. Metro Center, Inc., 267 NLRB 288, 114 LRRM 1215 (1983); Interlink Cable Systems, Inc., 121 LRRM 1354 (Advice Memorandum 1986).

74. Metropolitan Edison Co. v. NLRB, 460 U.S. 698, 112 LRRM 3265 (U.S. Sup. Ct. 1983). *See* Indiana & Michigan Electric Co., 273 NLRB 1540, 118 LRRM 1177 (1985), *enforced*, 786 F.2d 733, 121 LRRM 3259 (6th Cir. 1986) (no-strike clause requiring union to take action imposes obligations on stewards).

75. Atkinson v. Sinclair Refining Co., 370 U.S. 238, 50 LRRM 2433 (U.S. Sup. Ct. 1962) (strike called by union); Complete Auto Transit v. Reis, 451 U.S. 401, 107 LRRM 2145 (U.S. Sup. Ct. 1981) (wildcat strike).

76. Airco Speer Carbon Graphite v. IUE Local 502, 479 F.Supp. 246, 108 LRRM 2770 (W.D. Pa. 1979).

77. Mastro Plastics Corp. v. NLRB, 350 U.S. 270, 37 LRRM 2587(U.S. Sup. Ct. 1956); Arlan's Department Store, 133 NLRB 802, 48 LRRM 1731 (1961); Goodie Brand Packing Corp. 283 NLRB 673, 125 LRRM 1038 (1987).

Note: A union may, by explicit language in a no-strike clause, waive its right to conduct an unfair labor practice strike.

78. Spartan Equipment Co., 297 NLRB 19, 132 LRRM 1293 (1989).

79. Grandview Country Manor, Inc., 267 NLRB 1046, 114 LRRM 1103 (1983); Trinity Trucking Materials Corp., 221 NLRB 364, 90 LRRM 1499 (1975).

80. Hertz Corp., 297 NLRB 363, 133 LRRM 1046 (1989).

81. United Parcel Service 312 NLRB No. 103, 144 LRRM 1153 (1994).

82. Kime Plus, Inc., 295 NLRB 127, 133 LRRM 1007 (1989).

83. American Beef Packers, Inc. 193 NLRB 1117, 78 LRRM 1508 (1971).

84. *See* Shippers Dispatch, Inc., 223 NLRB 439, 92 LRRM 1252 (1976) (telling employee he is "stupid" for filing grievance, violation).

85. General Motors Corp., 232 NLRB 702, 107 LRRM 1606 (1981).

86. Progressive Building Methods, Inc., 262 NLRB 977, 110 LRRM 1398 (1982).

87. Daphne San Francisco Funeral Service, 224 NLRB 461, 92 LRRM 1590 (1976).

88. Lenkurt Electronic Co., Inc., 182 NLRB 510, 511, 74 LRRM 1182, 1184 (1970), *enforced*, 459 F.2d 635, 80 LRRM 2222 (9th Cir. 1972).

89. Painters District Council 2 v. Tiger Stripes, Inc., 582 F.Supp. 860, 117 LRRM 3021 (E.D. Mo. 1983); Local 744 v. Skokie Valley Beverage Co., 644 F.Sup. 213, 123 LRRM 3175 (N. Ill. 1986); Ohio Power Co., 45 LA 1034 (Leach, Arbitrator); B.P. Oil, Inc., 73 LA 347 (Berkowitz, Arbitrator).

90. Roadmaster Corp., 288 NLRB 1195, 129 LRRM 1008 (1988).

91. *See, e.g.*, Borg-Warner Corp., 102 NLRB 1223, 31 LRRM 1408 (1953); Russell Packing Co., 133 NLRB 194, 48 LRRM 1608 (1961); Market Basket, 144 NLRB 1462, 54 LRRM 1263 (1963). *Cf.* Trico Industries, Inc., 283 NLRB 848, 125 LRRM 1094 (1987) (in the absence of published rule, assumption that employer tolerates such activity unless it interferes with production or reaches disruptive levels).

92. Howmet Corp., 197 NLRB 471, 80 LRRM 1555 (1972).

93. Dow Chemical Co., 227 NLRB 1005, 94 LRRM 1697 (1977).

94. Circuit-Wise, Inc., 306 NLRB 766, 140 LRRM 1214 (1992).

95. Bethlehem Steel Co., 89 NLRB 341, 25 LRRM 1564 (1950).

96. Van Can Co., 304 NLRB 1085, n.5, 139 LRRM 1118, n.5 (1991).

97. Dow Chemical Co., 215 NLRB 910, 88 LRRM 1625 (1974), *enforcement denied on other grounds*, 536 F.2d 550, 92 LRRM 2545 (3rd Cir. 1976).

98. Dreis & Krump Mfg. Inc., 221 NLRB 309, 90 LRRM 1647 (1975).

99. Mitchell Manuals, 280 NLRB 230, 122 LRRM 1195 (1986).

100. Ralston Purina Co., 257 NLRB 601, 107 LRRM 1552 (1981).

101. Empire Steel Mfg. Co., 234 NLRB 530, 97 LRRM 1304 (1978).

102. Chrysler Corp., 228 NLRB 486, 94 LRRM 1508 (1977).

103. Mount Desert Island Hospital, 259 NLRB 589, 108 LRRM 1397 (1981).

104. Carpenters, Local 1098, 280 NLRB 875, 123 LRRM 1002 (1986).

105. Roadway Express, Inc., 241 NLRB 397, 100 LRRM 163 (1979).

106. Motorola Inc., 305 NLRB 580, 139 NLRB 1002 (1992) (T-shirt saying "just say no to drug testing," protected); Southern California Edison Co., 274 NLRB 1121, 119 LRRM 1051 (1985) (button, "Stick Your Retro," protected). **Note:** Buttons with extremely offensive, obnoxious, or obscene material may be denied protection under the Act. *See, e.g.* Southwestern Bell Telephone Co., 200 NLRB 667, 82 LRRM 1247 (1972) ("Ma Bell is a Cheap Mother," unprotected).

107. Clinton Foods, Inc., 237 NLRB 667, 99 LRRM 1043 (1978); Schneider's Dairy, Inc., 248 NLRB 1093, LRRM 1021 (1960). **Note:** An employer violates Section 8(a)(1) when its conduct tends to be coercive. Actual coercion is not necessary. Rockwell International Corp. v. NLRB, 814 F.2d 1530, 125 LRRM 2132 (11th Cir., 1987).

108. Universal Food Corp., 257 NLRB 702, 107 LRRM 1606 (1981).

109. General Motors Corp., 232 NLRB 335, 97 LRRM 1162 (1977).

110. Burgess Mining & Construction Corp., 250 NLRB 211, 104 LRRM 1548 (1980). *See also* Southern California Gas Co., 251 NLRB 922, 105 LRRM 1360 (1980) (telling employees that before presenting grievances to unions, they should bring problems to supervisor, violation).

111. *But see* General Fabrication Corp., 257 NLRB 219, 107 LRRM 1511 (1981) (company threat to lay off employees if union files grievance, violation).

112. United Telephone Co. of the West, 112 NLRB 779, 36 LRRM 1097 (1955).

113. Stevens & Associates Const. Co., 307 NLRB 1403, 141 LRRM 1253 (1992); Lear Siegler, Inc., 283 NLRB 929,

126 LRRM 1073 (1987) (mid-term changes in holiday and vacation provisions); Oak Cliff-Golman Baking Co., 207 NLRB 1063, 85 LRRM 1035 (1973) (reduction in wage rates).

114. Martinsburg Concrete Products Co., 248 NLRB 1352, 104 LRRM 1058 (1980); Indiana & Michigan Electric Co., 284 NLRB 53, 125 LRRM 1097 (1987).

115. *See* Teamsters, Local 238 v. C.R.S.T., Inc., 795 F.2d 1400, 122 LRRM 2993 (8th Cir. 1986). *But see* Paperworkers v. Wells Badger Industries, 124 LRRM 2658 (E.D. Wis. 1987) (intent to arbitrate post-contract discharges).

116. Circuit-Wise, Inc., 306 NLRB 766, 140 LRRM 1214 (1992).

117. Obie Pacific Inc., 196 NLRB 458, 80 LRRM 1169 (1972).

118. Max Factor & Co., 239 NLRB 804, 100 LRRM 1023 (1978).

119. Cook Paint & Varnish Co., 258 NLRB 1230, 1232, 108 LRRM 1150, 1152 (1981). *See also* Cook Paint & Varnish Co., 246 NLRB 646, 102 LRRM 1680 (1979).

120. *See, e.g.*, Service Technology Corp., 196 NLRB 845, 80 LRRM 1187 (1972); Primadonna Hotel, Inc., 165 NLRB 111, 65 LRRM 1423 (1967).

121. *See* Cook Paint & Varnish Co., 246 NLRB 646, 102 LRRM 1680 (1979) (threat to discharge two employees if they refused to respond to questions relating to grievance proceeding scheduled for arbitration, violation), *enforcement denied*, 648 F.2d 712, 106 LRRM 3016 (D.C. Cir. 1981); *decision after remand*, 258 NLRB 1230, 108 LRRM 1150 (1981); New Jersey Bell Telephone Co., 308 NLRB 277, 279, 141 LRRM 1017 (1992) (favorably citing rules enunciated in original Cook Paint & Varnish Co. decision). **Note:** According to the ALJ's opinion in Cook Paint & Varnish, employees

have a protected right to refuse to attend an arbitration proceeding despite the request of the employer (unless the employer has obtained and served a proper subpoena compelling attendance). 246 NLRB 646, 652 (1979).

122. Bill Scott Oldsmobile, 282 NLRB 1073, 124 LRRM 1161 (1987).

123. U.S. Postal Service, 252 NLRB 624, 105 LRRM 1308 (1980) (reinstating steward who refused an order to leave while a supervisor gave instructions to three recently disciplined employees). *Cf.* Garland Coal & Mining Co., 276 NLRB 963, 120 LRRM 1159 (1985) (union officer's refusal to obey order to sign company document, protected). *See also* International Harvester Co., 16 LA 307 (McKoy, Arbitrator). *But see* U.S. Postal Service, 268 NLRB 274, 114 LRRM 1291 (1983) (steward's refusal to obey reasonable order to quiet down, continuing to shout on shop floor, hurling insults, and disrupting operations, unprotected).

124. International Harvester Co., 16 LA 307 (McKoy, Arbitrator)

125. *See, e.g.*, Consolidated Freightways Corp. of Delaware, 257 NLRB 1281, 108 LRRM 1165 (1981); Northeast Constructors, 198 NLRB 846, 81 LRRM 1140 (1972); Cameron Ironworks Inc., 194 NLRB 168, 78 LRRM 1563 (1971), *enforced*, 464 F.2d 609, 80 LRRM 3369 (5th Cir. 1972).

126. Western Electric Co., Inc., 192 NLRB 556, 77 LRRM 1827 (1971).

127. *See* Essex International, 233 NLRB 1239, 97 LRRM 1115 (1977); Plough, Inc., 269 NLRB 129, 116 LRRM 1428 (1984).

128. Transit Union, Division 825, 240 NLRB 1267, 100 LRRM 1441 (1979).

129. Liberty Transfer Co., Inc., 218 NLRB 1117, 89 LRRM 1734 (1975). *See also* Oil Workers, Local 4-23, 274 NLRB 475, 118 LRRM 1432 (1985) (expulsion of supervisor/member, for testimony at arbitration, unlawful).

130. Ebasco Services, Inc., 181 NLRB 768, 73 LRRM 1518 (1970).

131. Pullman Trailmobile, 249 NLRB 430, 104 LRRM 1165 (1980).

132. U.S. Postal Service, 309 NLRB 13, 141 LRRM 1193 (1992); Wald Mfg. Co., 176 NLRB 839, 73 LRRM 1486 (1969) (making all grievances go to arbitration, violation).

133. Pennsylvania Telephone Guild, 277 NLRB 501, 120 LRRM 1257 (1985). *See* Kasser Distiller Products, 307 NLRB 899, 141 LRRM 1293 (1992) (refusal to sign severance package agreement, violation).

134. Signal Mfg. Co., 150 NLRB 1162, 58 LRRM 1202 (1965) *But see* Fitzsimons Mfg. Co., 251 NLRB 375, 105 LRRM 1083 (1980) (employer may refuse to deal with union representative who engaged in violent conduct).

135. Pennsylvania Telephone Guild, 277 NLRB 501, 120 LRRM 1257 (1985), *enforced*, 799 F.2d 84, 123 LRRM 2214 (3rd Cir. 1986).

136. Public Service Electric & Gas Co., 268 NLRB 361, 115 LRRM 1006 (1983).

137. *Id.*

138. *See* Bethlehem Steel Co., 89 NLRB 341, 25 LRRM 1564 (1950). *See also* U.S. Postal Service, 281 NLRB 1013, 123 LRRM 1209 (1986) (Section 9(a) applies to adjustments by EEO counselors).

139. Top Mfg. Co., 249 NLRB 424, 104 LRRM 1116 (1980).

140. B.C. Studios, Inc., 217 NLRB 307, 89 LRRM 1126 (1975); Laredo Packing Co., 254 NLRB 1, 106 LRRM 1350 (1981) (insisting that union drop lawsuit and unfair-labor-practice charge, violation).

141. Electromation, Inc., 309 NLRB 990, 142 LRRM 1001 (1992); E.I. du Pont de Nemours & Co., 311 NLRB 893, 143 LRRM 1121 (1993).

142. *See* AAA Voluntary Labor Arbitration Rules, Rule 27 (1987). *Compare* 29 CFR Section 1404.11 (FMCS).

143. United Steelworkers of America v. Warrior & Gulf Navigation Co., 363 U.S. 574, 46 LRRM 2416 (U.S. Sup. Ct. 1960). *See* AT&T Technologies, Inc. v. CWA, 475 U.S. 643, 121 LRRM 3329 (U.S. Sup. Ct. 1986). Suit must be filed within six months from date employer refuses to arbitrate.

144. Mid-American Milling Co., 282 NLRB 926, 124 LRRM 1209 (1987). *But see* American Beef Packers, Inc., 193 NLRB 1117, 78 LRRM 1508 (1971) (refusal to process three grievances, delay in processing eight grievances, Section 8(a)(5) violation).

145. Edna H. Pagel, Inc. v. Teamsters Local 595, 667 F.2d 1275, 109 LRRM 2663 (9th Cir. 1982). **Note:** Employer appeals seeking to vacate arbitration awards are also disfavored. *See* United Paperworkers Union v. Misco, Inc., 484 U.S. 29, 126 LRRM 3113 (U.S. Sup. Ct. 1987). (reviewing courts are not authorized to reconsider the merits of an arbitration award).

146. L.A. Newspaper Guild v. Hearst Corp., 504 F.2d 636, 87 LRRM 2597 (9th Cir. 1974) (arbitrator incorrectly ruled union's grievances non-arbitrable).

147. Southern California Edison Co., 274 NLRB 1121, 119 LRRM 1051 (1985)(button must not be obscene).

148. Allied Aviation Service Co., 248 NLRB 229, 103 LRRM 1455 (1980).

149. St. Lukes Hospital, 300 NLRB 836, 135 LRRM 1289 (1990).

150. Tri-County Medical Center, 222 NLRB 1089, 91 LRRM 1323 (1976).

151. John S. Swift Co., Inc., 124 NLRB 394, 44 LRRM 1388 (1954); Honolulu Rapid Transit Co., Ltd., 110 NLRB 1806, 35 LRRM 1305 (1944). *But see* Lodge 76 Machinists v. Wisconsin Employment Relations

Commission, 427 U.S. 132, 92 LRRM 2881 (U.S. Sup. Ct. 1976) (raising possibility that partial strikes may be protected).

152. Dow Chemical Co., 152 NLRB 1150, 59 LRRM 1279 (1965). *See also* Paperworkers Local 5, 294 NLRB 779, n. 17, 131 LRRM 1545, n. 17 (1989) (refusals to perform voluntary work do not violate no-strike clauses).

153. U.S. Postal Service, 280 NLRB 685, 122 LRRM 1337 (1986).

154. NLRB v. Acme Industrial Co., 385 U.S. 432, 64 LRRM 2069 (U.S. Sup. Ct. 1967).

155. United Graphic Inc., 281 NLRB 463, 123 LRRM 1097 (1986).

156. General Motors Corp., 253 NLRB 186, 101 LRRM 1461 (1979), *enforced as modified*, 648 F.2d 18, 105 LRRM 3337 (D.C. Cir. 1980).

157. New York Telephone Co., 299 NLRB 351, 135 LRRM 1051 (1990).

158. Hercules, Inc., 281 NLRB 961, 124 LRRM 1213 (1986), *enforced*, 833 F.2d 426, 126 LRRM 3187 (2nd Cir. 1987).

159. The New York Times Co., 265 NLRB 353, 111 LRRM 1578 (1982).

160. General Motors Corp., 243 NLRB 186, 101 LRRM 1461 (1979).

161. Southeastern Brush Co., 306 NLRB 884, 140 LRRM 1164 (1992).

162. U.S. Postal Service, 276 NLRB 1282, 120 LRRM 1277 (1985).

163. Safeway Stores, Inc., 236 NLRB 1126, 98 LRRM 1397 (1978), *enforced*, 622 F.2d 425, 104 LRRM 2765 (9th Cir. 1980).

164. C. & P. Telephone Co., 259 NLRB 225, 109 LRRM 1019 (1981).

165. T.U. Electric, 306 NLRB 654, 140 LRRM 1116 (1992).

166 *Id.*

167. Detroit Edison Co. v. NLRB, 440 U.S. 301, 100 LRRM 2728 (U.S. Sup. Ct. 1979). *See* Washington Gas Light Co., 273 NLRB 116, 118 LRRM 1001 (1984).

168. Colgate-Palmolive Co., 261 NLRB 90, 94, 109 LRRM 1352, 1357 (1982), *enforced*, 711 F.2d 348, 113 LRRM 3163 (D.C. Cir. 1983).

169. Oil, Chemical & Atomic Workers v. NLRB, 711 F.2d 348, 113 LRRM 3163 (D.C. Cir. 1983).

170. U.S. Postal Service, 308 NLRB 547, 141 LRRM 1118 (1992) (four-week delay in producing attendance records, violation).

171. ITT Continental Baking Co., 103 LRRM 1499 (Advice Memorandum 1980).

172. L.M. Settles Construction Co., Inc., 259 NLRB 379, 108 LRRM 1380 (1981).

173. Hawkins Construction Co., Inc., 285 NLRB 1313, 1315, 126 LRRM 1251 (1987), *enforcement denied on other grounds*, 857 F.2d 1224, 129 LRRM 2486 (1988).

174. Pfizer, Inc., 268 NLRB 916, 115 LRRM 1105 (1984), *enforced*, 763 F.2d 887, 119 LRRM 2947 (7th Cir. 1985).

175. *See* Washington Gas Light Co., 273 NLRB 116, 118 LRRM 1001 (1984).

176. Goodyear Atomic Corp., 266 NLRB 890, 113 LRRM 1057 (1983), *enforced*, 738 F.2d 155, 116 LRRM 3023 (6th Cir. 1984); Minnesota Mining & Mfg. Co., 261 NLRB 27, 109 LRRM 1345 (1982), *enforced*, 711 F.2d 348, 113 LRRM 3163(D.C. Cir. 1983); Tower Books, 273 NLRB 671, 118 LRRM 1113 (1984).

177. Food Employer Council, Inc., 187 NLRB 651, 80 LRRM 1440 (1972).

178. American Telephone & Telegraph Co., 250 NLRB 47, 104 LRRM 1381 (1980).

179. American Cyanamid Co., 124 NLRB 683, 44 LRRM 1587 (1959); *but see* Westinghouse Electric Corp., 239 NLRB 106, 99 LRRM 1482 (1978) (employer must present information to union in a reasonable, clear, and understandable format).

180. New York Telephone Co., 299 NLRB 351, 135 LRRM 1051 (1990), *enforced,* 930 F.2d 1005, 137 LRRM 2123 (2nd Cir. 1991).

181. General Motors Corp., 243 NLRB 186, 101 LRRM 1461 (1979), *enforced as modified,* 648 F.2d 18, 105 LRRM 3337 (D.C. Cir. 1980).

182. C & P Telephone Co., 259 NLRB 225, 109 LRRM 1019 (1981), *enforced,* 687 F.2d 633, 111 LRRM 2165 (2nd Cir. 1982).

183. Pfizer, Inc., 268 NLRB 916, 115 LRRM 1105 (1984), *enforced,* 763 F.2d 887, 119 LRRM 2947 (7th Cir. 1985). *See* Culinary Workers Union, Local 226, 281 NLRB 284, 124 LRRM 1142 (1986) (union has right to arbitration awards involving other unions with similar contract language).

184. U.S. Postal Service, 310 NLRB 391, 142 LRRM 1233 (1993).

185. Lukens Steel Co., 42 LA 849 (Crawford, Arbitrator).

186. Detroit Edison Co. v. NLRB, 440 U.S. 301, 100 LRRM 2728 (U.S. Sup. Ct. 1979).

187. Holyoke Water Power Co., 273 NLRB 1369, 118 LRRM 1179 (1985) *enforced,* 778 F.2d 49, 120 LRRM 3487 (1st Cir. 1985).

188. New England Tel. & Tel. Co., 309 NLRB 558, 142 LRRM 1325 (1992); Fairmont Hotel, 304 NLRB 746, 139 LRRM 1133 (1991) (name of complaining guest).

189. *Id.*

190. U.S. Postal Service, 306 NLRB 474, 140 LRRM 1136 (1992) (drug informant). *See* Pennsylvania Power & Light Co., 301 NLRB 1104, 136 LRRM 1225 (1991) (confidentiality claim forecloses employer's ability to use witness at arbitration hearing).

191. Mobil Oil Corp. 303 NLRB 780, 137 LRRM 1361 (1991).

192. Anheuser-Busch Inc., 237 NLRB 982, 99 LRRM 1174 (1974). *But see* T. U. Electric, 306 NLRB 654, 140 LRRM 1116 (1992) (supervisor's notes not witness statements).

193. WCCO Radio, Inc., 282 NLRB 159, 125 LRRM 1046 (1987) (rejecting trade secret and confidentiality defenses). *See* The Patriot News Co., 308 NLRB 1296, 142 LRRM 1231 (1992) (amounts of Christmas bonuses).

194. Minnesota Mining & Mfg. Co., 261 NLRB 27, 109 LRRM 1345 (1982), *enforced*, 711 F.2d 348, 113 LRRM 3163 (D.C. Cir. 1983); Plough, Inc., 262 NLRB 1095, 111 LRRM 1013 (1982). *See also* 29 CFR §1910.20 (OSHA rule allowing union, with written authorizations, to obtain medical records of employees and records of toxic exposures). The OSHA rule can be used irrespective of whether a grievance has been filed or is contemplated.

195. Minnesota Mining & Mfg. Co., *Id.*

196. Columbus Maintenance & Service Co., 269 NLRB 198, 115 LRRM 1233 (1984).

197. Litton Systems, Inc., 283 NLRB 973, 125 LRRM 1081 (1987) (studies and analysis relating to relocation decision); General Dynamics Corp., 268 NLRB 1432, 115 LRRM 1199 (1984).

198. New England Tel. & Tel. Co., 309 NLRB 558, 142 LRRM 1325 (1992); United Technologies Corp., 277 NLRB 584, 121 LRRM 1290 (1985).

199. New Jersey Bell Telephone Co., 300 NLRB 42, 135 LRRM 1241 (1990).

200. Designcraft Jewel Industries, Inc., 254 NLRB 791, 107 LRRM 1034 (1981), *enforced*, 675 F.2d 493, 109 LRRM 3341 (2nd Cir. 1982).

201. ACF Industries, Inc., 231 NLRB 83, 96 LRRM 1291 (1977), *enforced*, 592 F.2d 422, 100 LRRM 2710 (8th Cir. 1974).

202. Minnesota Mining & Mfg. Co., 261 NLRB 35, 109 LRRM 1345 (1982).

203. IUE v. NLRB, 648 F.2d 18, 28, 105 LRRM 3337 (D.C. Cir. 1980).

204. First National Maintenance Corp. v. NLRB, 452 U.S. 666, 107 LRRM 2705 (U.S. Sup. Ct. 1981).

205. BC Industries, Inc., 307 NLRB 1275, 140 LRRM 1326 (1992).

206. Dubuque Packing Co., 303 NLRB 386, 137 LRRM 1185 (1991).

207. *See* Show Industries, Inc. 312 NLRB No. 84, 145 LRRM 1293 (1994).

208. Seiler Tank Truck Service, 307 NLRB 1090, 141 LRRM 1283 (1992).

209. 5 U.S.C. §552a.

210. U.S. Postal Service, 310 NLRB 391, 142 LRRM 1233 (1993).

211. Plasterers Local No. 346, 273 NLRB 1143, 118 LRRM 124 (1984).

212. NLRB v. J. Weingarten, Inc., 420 U.S. 251, 88 LRRM 2689 (U.S. Sup. Ct. 1975).

213. Baton Rouge Water Works Co., 246 NLRB 995, 103 LRRM 1056 (1979).

214. Pacific Telephone & Telegraph Co., 262 NLRB 1048, 110 LRRM 1411 (1982), *enforced in part*, 711 F.2d 134, 113 LRRM 3529 (9th Cir. 1983).

215. U.S. Postal Service, 303 NLRB 463, 138 LRRM 1339 (1991).

216. Southwestern Bell Telephone Co., 251 NLRB 612, 105 LRRM 1246 (1980).

217. New Jersey Bell Telephone Co., 308 NLRB 277, 141 LRRM 1017 (1992).

218. U.S. Postal Service, 288 NLRB 864, 130 LRRM 1184 (1988).

219. NLRB v. J. Weingarten, Inc., 420 U.S. 251, 260, 88 LRRM 2689 (U.S. Sup. Ct. 1975).

220. New Jersey Bell Telephone Co., 308 NLRB 277, 141 LRRM 1017 (1992).

221. NLRB v. J. Weingarten, Inc., 420 U.S. 251, 88 LRRM 2689 (U.S. Sup. Ct. 1975).

222. Miranda v. Arizona, 384 U.S. 436 (1966).

223. Amoco Oil Co., 278 NLRB 1, 121 LRRM 1308 (1986).

224. ILGWU v. Quality Mfg. Co., 420 U.S. 276, 88 LRRM 2698 (U.S. Sup. Ct. 1975).

225. Appalachian Power Co., 253 NLRB 931, 106 LRRM 1041 (1980). **Note:** An employee's silence, after a steward asks to be present, may be considered agreement with the request. *See* Colgate Palmolive Co., 257 NLRB 130, 107 LRRM 1486 (1981).

226. Southwestern Bell Telephone Co., 227 NLRB 1223, 94 LRRM 1305 (1977).

227. Joseph F. Whelan Co., 273 NLRB 340, 118 LRRM 1040 (1984); Roadway Express, 246 NLRB 1127, 103 LRRM 1050 (1979).

228. Glomac Plastics, Inc., 234 NLRB 1309, 97 LRRM 1441 (1977), *enforced*, 592 F.2d 94, 100 LRRM 2508 (2nd Cir. 1979); Interstate Security Services, Inc., 263 NLRB 6, 110 LRRM 1535 (1982).

229. U.S. Postal Service, 252 NLRB 61, 105 LRRM 1200 (1980).

230. Consolidated Casinos Corp., 266 NLRB 988, 113 LRRM 1081 (1983).

231. *See* Safeway Stores, 303 NLRB 989, 138 LRRM 1007 (1991) (discharge for refusal to take drug test, after denial of union representation, violation). *See also* System 99, 289 NLRB 723, 131 LRRM 1226 (1988) (sobriety test).

232. *See* E.I. du Pont de Nemours & Co., 100 LRRM 1633 (Advice Memorandum 1981) (car search); Chrysler Corp. (Advice Memorandum 1981) (cited in Walnut Hill Convalescent Home, 114 LRRM 1255 (Advice Memorandum 1983) (handbag search)).

233. Good Hope Refineries, 245 NLRB 380, 102 LRRM 1302 (1979).

234. Amoco Chemicals Corp., 237 NLRB 394, 99 LRRM 1017 (1978).

235. *See* Baton Rouge Water Works, Inc., 246 NLRB 995, 103 LRRM 1056 (1979). Although an employer can insist that an employee sign a warning slip without a union representative, an employer cannot take action against an employee because the employee makes a request for the assistance of a union representative prior to signing. U.S. Postal Service, 237 NLRB 1104, 99 LRRM 1179 (1978) (Section 7 provides right to seek support of union representative), *enforcement denied on other grounds*, 614 F.2d 384, 103 LRRM 2693 (4th Cir. 1980). **Note:** If by past practice, stewards have been called in when employees receive warnings, management must continue to abide by this practice. *See* Westinghouse Electric Corp., 243 NLRB 306, 101 LRRM 1497 (1979).

236. TCC Center Companies, 275 NLRB 604, 119 LRRM 1195 (1985).

237. Pacific Southwest Airlines, 242 NLRB 1169, 101 LRRM 1366 (1979).

238. Baton Rouge Water Works, Inc., 246 NLRB 995, 103 LRRM 1056 (1979).

239. Coca-Cola Bottling Co., 227 NLRB 1276, 94 LRRM 1200 (1977).

240. Keystone Consolidated Industries, Inc., 217 NLRB 995, 89 LRRM 1192 (1975).

241. Northwest Engineering Co., 265 NLRB 190, 111 LRRM 148 (1982).

242. Kraft Foods, Inc., 251 NLRB 598, 105 LRRM 1233 (1980).

243. Taracorp, Inc., 273 NLRB 221, 117 LRRM 1497 (1984).

244. Safeway Stores, 303 NLRB 989, 138 LRRM 1007 (1991).

245. *See* Pennsylvania Telephone Guild, 255 NLRB 976, 120 LRRM 1257 (1985), *enforced*, 799 F.2d 84, 123 LRRM 2214 (3rd Cir. 1986).

246. Consolidated Coal Co., 307 NLRB 976, 140 LRRM 1248 (1992).

247. Johnson-Bateman Co., 295 NLRB 180, 131 LRRM 1393 (1989).

248. Alamo Cement Co., 277 NLRB 1031, 121 LRRM 1131 (1985).

249. Hi-Tech Cable Corp., 309 NLRB 3, 142 LRRM 1338 (1992).

250. *Id.* (management-rights clause giving employer sole right to make, change, and enforce "reasonable rules", not waiver of union's right to bargain over no-tobacco-usage rule); Johnson-Bateman Co., 295 NLRB 180, 131 LRRM 1393 (1989) (drug and alcohol testing policy, not covered by management-rights clause).

251. Owens Corning Fiberglas, 282 NLRB 609, 124 LRRM 1105 (1987); Johnson-Bateman Co., 295 NLRB 180, 131 LRRM 1393 (1989).

252. Ciba-Geigy Pharmaceuticals Div., 264 NLRB 1013, 111 LRRM 1460 (1982).

253. Concord Docu-Prep, Inc., 207 NLRB 981, 85 LRRM 1416 (1973).

254. G.J. Aigner Co., 257 NLRB 669, 107 LRRM 1586 (1981).

255. *See* Randolph Children's Home, 309 NLRB 341, 143 LRRM 1010 (1992).

256. Santa Rosa Blueprint Service, Inc., 288 NLRB 762, 130 LRRM 1403 (1988); Brown & Connolly, Inc., 237 NLRB 271, 98 LRRM 1572 (1978).

257. Johnson-Bateman Co., 295 NLRB 180, 131 LRRM 1393 (1989).

258. Ford Motor Co. v. NLRB, 441 U.S. 488, 101 LRRM 2222 (U.S. Sup. Ct. 1979); E.I. du Pont de Nemours & Co., 269 NLRB 24, 115 LRRM 1192 (1982).

259. Hanes Corp., 260 NLRB 557, 109 LRRM 1185 (1982). *See also* Armour Oil Co., 253 NLRB 1104, 106 LRRM 1127 (1981) (decision to replace trucks with vehicles more difficult to handle and lacking safety equipment must be bargained); Winona Industries, Inc., 257 NLRB 695, 107 LRRM 1605 (1981) (rule prohibiting employees from wearing "tank tops" for safety reasons, mandatory topic).

260. Caterpillar Inc., 321 NLRB 1178, 1182, 153 LRRM 1058 (1996). *See also* Intermountain Rural Electric Ass'n, 305 NLRB 783, 787-88, 139 LRRM 1003 (1991), *enforced*, 984 F. 2d 1562, 142 LRRM 2448 (10th Cir. 1993).

261. Hyatt Regency Memphis, 296 NLRB 259, 263-4 (1989); *enforced*, 939 F. 2d 361, 138 LRRM 2115 (6th Cir. 1991).

262. Champion Parts Rebuilders, Inc., 260 NLRB 731, 109 LRRM 1220 (1982), *enforcement denied in part*, 717 F.2d 845, 114 LRRM 2674 (3rd Cir. 1983) (on grounds that a single refusal to allow use of company photocopy machine does not constitute a new policy).

263. Howmet Corp., 197 NLRB 471, 80 LRRM 1555 (1972).

264. The Mead Corp., 256 NLRB 686, 107 LRRM 1309 (1981).

265. Furniture Rentors Inc., 311 NLRB 749, 143 LRRM 1249 (1993).

266. Southern California Edison Co., 284 NLRB 1205, 126 LRRM 1324 (1987). *See also* Jones Dairy Farm, 295 NLRB 113, 131 LRRM 1487 (1989) (new policy requiring injured employees to enter work hardening program, mandatory bargaining subject).

267. Dilene Answering Service, 257 NLRB 284, n.6, 107 LRRM 1490, n. 6 (1981).

268. Lapeer Foundry, 289 NLRB 952, 954, 129 LRRM 1001 (1988).

269. Mercy Hospital, 311 NLRB 1159, 143 LRRM 1295 (1993).

270. Standard Candy Co. 147 NLRB 1070, 56 LRRM 1316 (1964) (increase in minimum wage); Murphy Oil USA, 286 NLRB 1039, 127 LRRM 1111 (1987) (coming into compliance with OSHA standard, no bargaining requirement according to ALJ).

271. *See* Murphy Oil USA, *Id.*; Architectural Fiberglass, 165 NLRB 241, 65 LRRM 1332 (1967).

272. Furniture Rentors, Inc., 311 NLRB 749, 143 LRRM 1249 (1993).

273. U.S. Postal Service, 302 NLRB 918, 137 LRRM 1352 (1991).

274. *See* ITT Continental Baking Co., 103 LRRM 1499 (Advice Memorandum 1980).

275. *See* Akron Brass Co., 93 LA 1070 (Shanker, Arbitrator) (all-inclusive no-smoking policy, unreasonable).

276. Vaca v. Sipes, 386 U.S. 171, 190, 64 LRRM 2369, 2376 (U.S. Sup. Ct. 1967).

277. SEIU, Local 579, 229 NLRB 692, 695, 95 LRRM 1156 (1977).

278. Bowen v. United States Postal Service, 459 U.S. 212, 112 LRRM 2281 (U.S. Sup. Ct. 1983).

279. See Pacific Northwest Bell Telephone Co., 110 LRRM 1559 (Advice Memorandum 1982).

280. *See* Goodman v. Lukens Steel Co., 482 U.S. 656 (U.S. Sup. Ct. 1987).

281. U.S. Postal Service, 310 NLRB 599, 142 LRRM 1342 (1993). *See also* Furniture Workers Local 282, 291 NLRB 182, 129 LRRM 1334 (1988) (union may not charge nonmembers special fee to process grievances).

282. Shane v. Greyhound Lines, 868 F.2d 1057, 130 LRRM 2822 (9th Cir. 1989).

283. Hotel & Restaurant Employees, Local 64, 278 NLRB 773, 121 LRRM 1283 (1986).

284. *See* Israel, Stuart, Litigating Grievance Arbitrations, *The Practical Litigator*, March 1993, p. 60.

285. Stevens v. Moore Business Forms, 145 LRRM 2668 (9th Cir. 1994).

286. Local 13 v. Pacific Maritime Asso., 441 F.2d 1061, 77 LRRM 2160 (9th Cir. 1971). *See* IUE, Local 801, 100 LRRM 1385 (Advice Memorandum 1979), Berrigan v. Greyhound Lines, Inc., 782 F.2d 295, 121 LRRM 2510 (1st Cir. 1986).

287. Newspaper Guild, Local 35, 239 NLRB 1321, 100 LRRM 1179 (1979). *But see* Smith v. Hussman Refrigerator Co., 619 F.2d 1229, 103 LRRM 2321 (8th Cir. 1980) (union policy of evaluating promotion grievances based only on seniority, without consideration of skill or ability, DFR violation). **Note:** In cases of conflicting claims, the union should keep the employee it is grieving against informed of the grievance and arbitration hearings, and consider allowing the employee to have an opportunity to present a position at the hearings. *See generally*, Smith v. Hussman Refrigerator Co., *supra*; Larry v. Penn Truck Aids, Inc., 112 LRRM 2949 (E.D. Pa. 1982) (lack of notice resulting in no representation of adversely affected employee's interests, actionable DFR breach).

288. Painters, Local 310, 270 NLRB 506, 116 LRRM 1099 (1984).

289. *See* Clerks and Checkers, Local 1593, 234 NLRB 511, 98 LRRM 1328 (1978).

290. Fritz v. Production Plated Plastics, Inc., 676 F.Supp. 148, 125 LRRM 3452 (W.D. Mich. 1987). *See also* Encina v. Tony Lama Boot Co., 448 F.2d 1264, 78 LRRM 2382 (5th Cir. 1971) (in grievance of doubtful validity, union permitted to condition arbitration on grievant's paying the costs).

291. *See* Mahnke v. WERC, 103 LRRM 2313 (Wisconsin Cir. Ct. 1979).

292. Tongay v. Kroger Co., 860 F.2d 298, 129 LRRM 2752 (8th Cir. 1988).

293. Freeman v. Teamsters Local 135, 746 F.2d 1316, 117 LRRM 2873 (7th Cir. 1984). *See also* Sear v. Cadillac Automobile Co., 654 F.2d 4, 107 LRRM 3218 (1st Cir. 1981) (suggesting that DFR claim should only be allowed "in unusual instances where unfairness is blatant"). **Note:** A union may be held liable if it fails to go to court to seek enforcement of an arbitrator's decision which favors employees. *See* Samples v. Ryder Truck Lines, Inc., 755 F.2d 881, 118 LRRM 3233 (11th Cir. 1985). Enforcement actions must be filed within six months from the arbitrator's award. *Id.*

294. DelCostello v. Teamsters, 462 U.S. 151, 113 LRRM 2737 (U.S. Sup. Ct. 1983).

295. Suwanchai v. IBEW, Local 1973, 528 F. Supp. 851, 112 LRRM 2050 (D.N.H. 1981).

296. Dairylea Cooperative, Inc., 219 NLRB 656, 89 LRRM 1737 (1975), *enforced*, 531 F.2d 1162, 91 LRRM 2929 (2nd Cir. 1976).

297. Gulton Electro-Voice, 266 NLRB 406, 112 LRRM 1361 (1983) (dropping presumption of legality for union officers), *enforced*, 727 F.2d 1184, 115 LRRM 2760 (D.C. Cir. 1984).

298. Teamsters, Local 633, 230 NLRB 81, 96 LRRM 1096 (1977).

299. BASF Wyandotte Corp., 274 NLRB 978, 119 LRRM 1035 (1985); BASF Wyandotte v. ICWU Local 227, 791 F.2d 1046, 122 LRRM 2750 (2nd Cir. 1986).

300. *Id.*, 791 F.2d at 1050, 122 LRRM at 2753.

301. National Fuel Gas Distribution Corp., 308 NLRB 841, 141 LRRM 1097 (1992) (relying in part on Toth v. USX Corp., 883 F.2d 1297, 132 LRRM 2275 (7th Cir. 1989). *But see* Trailways Lines, Inc. v. Amalgamated Transit Union, 785 F.2d. 101, 121 LRRM 3167 (3rd Cir. 1986).

302. UAW, Local 1331, 228 NLRB 1446, 95 LRRM 1071 (1977). *But see* Laborers, Local 380, 275 NLRB 1049, 120 LRRM 1023 (1985) (union unable to show need for steward's presence on weekends and holidays).

303. IUE, Local 663, 276 NLRB 1043, 120 LRRM 1150 (1985).

304. UAW, Local 561, 266 NLRB 952 n. 9, 113 LRRM 1065 n. 9 (1983).

305. Wayne Corp., 270 NLRB No. 28, 116 LRRM 1049 (1984), *enforced*, 776 F.2d 745, 120 LRRM 3321 (7th Cir. 1985) (occasional performance of steward-like duties on a substitute basis not sufficient to legitimize superseniority).

306. IUE, Local 663, 276 NLRB 1043, 120 LRRM 1150 (1985).

307. Otis Elevator Co., 231 NLRB 1128, 1130 n.4, 96 LRRM 1108, 1110 n.4 (1977).

308. Teamsters Local 293, 311 NLRB 538, 143 LRRM 1237 (1993).

309. Frankline Inc., 287 NLRB 263, 127 LRRM 1132 (1987).

310. 29 U.S.C. §401, *et seq.*

311. 29 U.S.C. §504a. **Note:** This section also bars persons who are, or have been, members of the Communist Party from union posts. This part of the statute was ruled

unconstitutional by the Supreme Court in U.S. v. Brown, 381 U.S. 437, 59 LRRM 2353 (1965).

312. 21 U.S.C. §802(16).

313. Finnegan v. Leu, 456 U.S. 431, 441, 110 LRRM 2321, 2324 (U.S. Sup. Ct. 1982) (removal of business agent). *See* Purdie v. Vinson, 144 LRRM 2871 (S.D.N.Y. 1993) (preliminary injunction restoring steward to position since appointed steward's removal was part of a pattern of repression of members' free speech rights).

314. Sheet Metal Workers v. Lynn, 488 U.S. 347, 130 LRRM 2193 (U.S. Sup. Ct. 1989).

315. 29 U.S.C. §481. "Officer" is defined in 29 U.S.C. §402(n).

316. 29 U.S.C. §502(a).

317. Plumbers and Pipefitters, Local 520, 282 NLRB 1228, 124 LRRM 1281 (1987). *See also* Painters District Council No. 2, 239 NLRB 1378, 100 LRRM 1152 (1979) (union can refer steward to job even if this requires layoff of already-hired worker), *enforcement denied*, 620 F.2d 1326, 104 LRRM 2368 (8th Cir. 1980).

318. John P. Bell & Sons, Inc., 266 NLRB 607, 112 LRRM 1425 (1983).

319. Aces Mechanical Corp., 282 NLRB 928, 124 LRRM 1145 (1987).

320. Bethenergy Mines, Inc. 308 NLRB 1242, 141 LRRM 1145 (1992).

321. Monks Inn, Inc., 232 NLRB 978, 97 LRRM 1249 (1977); Cooper-Jarrett, Inc., 260 NLRB 1123, 109 LRRM 1265 (1982).

322. 29 U.S.C. §201 *et. seq.*

323. *See* 29 CFR §§778.115 and 29 CFR §778.419.

324. Donovan v. Williams Chemical Co., 682 F.2d 185 (5th Cir. 1982).

325. 29 U.S.C. §2611 *et. seq.*

326. 29 U.S.C. §651 *et. seq.*

327. 29 CFR §1977.12(b).

328. 49 U.S.C. app. §2305(b) (Surface Transportation Assistance Act — enforced by filing a complaint with OSHA).

329. 29 U.S.C. §143.

330. 42 U.S.C. §2000e *et. seq.*

331. 42 U.S.C. §12101 *et. seq.*

332. 29 U.S.C. §621, *et. seq.*

333. 40 U.S.C. §276a.

334. 29 U.S.C. §2001.

335. 29 U.S.C. §1001, *et. seq.*

336. 29 U.S.C. §206(d)(1).

337. 8 U.S.C. §1186.

338. 29 U.S.C. §401 *et. seq.*

339. 41 U.S.C. §35 *et. seq.*

340. 29 U.S.C. §2101 *et. seq.*

APPENDIX: National Labor Relations Board Offices

REGION 1 (Maine, Massachusetts, New Hampshire, Rhode Island, Vermont)

Federal Building, 6th Floor
10 Causeway Street
Boston, MA 02222
Tel: (617) 565-6700
Rosemary Pye, Regional Director

REGION 2 (New York)

Federal Building, Room 3614
26 Federal Plaza
New York, N.Y. 10278
Tel: (212) 264-0300
Daniel A. Silverman, Regional Director

REGION 3 (New York)

Federal Building, Room 901
111 West Huron Street
Buffalo, NY 14202
Tel: (716) 846-4931
Richard L. Ahearn, Regional Director

Resident Office:

Federal Building, Room 342
Clinton Avenue at North Pearl Street
Albany, N.Y. 12207
Tel: (518) 472-2215

REGION 4 (Delaware, New Jersey, Pennsylvania)

One Independence Mall, 7th Floor
615 Chestnut Street
Philadelphia, PA 19106
Tel: (215) 597-7601
Peter W. Hirsch, Regional Director

REGION 5 (Delaware, D.C., Maryland, Pennsylvania, Virginia, West Virginia)

Candler Building, 4th Floor
103 South Gay Street
Baltimore, MD 21202
Tel: (410) 962-2822
Louis J. D'Amico, Regional Director

Resident Office:

Gelman Building, Suite 100
2120 L Street N.W.
Washington, D.C. 20037
Tel: (202) 254-7612

REGION 6 (Pennsylvania, West Virginia)

Federal Building, Room 1501
1000 Liberty Avenue
Pittsburgh, PA 15222
Tel: (412) 395-4400
Gerald Kobell, Regional Director

REGION 7 (Michigan)

Federal Building, Room 300
477 Michigan Avenue
Detroit, MI 48226
Tel: (313) 226-3200
William C. Schaub, Jr., Regional Director

REGION 8 (Ohio)

Federal Building, Suite 1695
1240 East Ninth Street
Cleveland, OH 44199
Tel: (216) 522-3715
Frederick J. Calatrello, Regional Director

REGION 9 (Indiana, Kentucky, Ohio, West Virginia)

Federal Building, Room 3003
550 Main Street
Cincinnati, OH 45202
Tel: (513) 684-3686
Richard L. Ahearn, Regional Director

REGION 10 (Alabama, Georgia, Tennessee)

Marietta Tower, Suite 2400
101 Marietta Street, N.W.
Atlanta, GA 30323
Tel: (404) 331-2896
Martin A. Arlook, Regional Director

Resident Office:

2025 Third Avenue North
Birmingham, AL 35203
Tel: (205) 731-1062

REGION 11 (North Carolina, South Carolina, Tennessee, Virginia, West Virginia)

U.S. Courthouse and Federal Building, Room 447
251 North Main Street
Winston-Salem, NC 27101
Tel: (910) 631-5201
William Lee Clark, Jr., Regional Director

REGION 12 (Florida, Georgia)

201 East Kennedy Boulevard
Tampa, FL 33602
Tel: (813) 228-2641
Rochelle Kentov, Regional Director

Resident Offices:

Federal Building, Room 916
51 Southwest First Avenue
Miami, FL 33130
Tel: (305) 536-5391

Federal Building, Room 278
400 West Bay Street
Jacksonville, FL 32202
Tel: (904) 232-3768

REGION 13 (Illinois, Indiana)

200 West Adams Street
Chicago, IL 60606
Tel: (312) 353-7570
Elizabeth Kinney, Regional Director

REGION 14 (Illinois, Missouri)

611 North 10th Street, Room 400
St. Louis, MO 63101
Tel: (314) 425-4167
Ralph R. Tremain, Regional Director

REGION 15 (Alabama, Florida, Louisiana, Mississippi)

1515 Poydras Street, Room 610
New Orleans, LA 70112
Tel: (504) 589-6361
H. Frank Malone, Regional Director

REGION 16 (Arkansas, Texas)

Federal Office Building, Room 8-A-24
819 Taylor Street
Fort Worth, TX 76102
Tel: (817) 334-2921
Michael Dunn, Regional Director

Resident Office:

440 Louisiana Street, Suite 550
Houston, TX 77002
Tel: (713) 238-9632

REGION 17 (Iowa, Kansas, Missouri, Nebraska)

5799 Broadmoor, Suite 500
Mission, KS 66202
Tel: (913) 236-3000
F. Rozier Sharp, Regional Director

Resident Office:

Cranston Building, Suite 900
111 W. 5th Street
Tulsa, OK 74101

REGION 18 (Iowa, Minnesota, North Dakota, South Dakota, Wisconsin)

Federal Building, Room 316
110 South 4th Street
Minneapolis, MN 55401
Tel: (612) 348-1757
Ronald M. Sharp, Regional Director

Resident Office:

210 Walnut Street, Room 909
Des Moines, IA 50309
Tel: (515) 284-4391

REGION 19 (Alaska, Idaho, Montana, Oregon, Washington)

Federal Building, Room 2948
915 Second Avenue
Seattle, WA 98174
Tel: (206) 220-6300
John D. Nelson, Regional Director

Resident Office:

Federal Office Building, Room 21
222 West Seventh Avenue
Anchorage, AK 99513
Tel: (907) 271-5015

Sub-Regional Office:

222 S.W. Columbia
Portland, OR 97201
Tel: (503) 326-3085

REGION 20 (California, Hawaii)

901 Market Street, Room 400
San Francisco, CA 94103
Tel: (415) 744-6810
Robert H. Miller, Regional Director

Sub-Regional Office:

300 Ala Moana Boulevard, Room 7318
Honolulu, HI 96850
Tel: (808) 541-2814

REGION 21 (California)

888 South Figueroa Street, Ninth Floor
Los Angeles, CA 90017
Tel: (213) 894-5200
Victoria E. Aguayo, Regional Director

Resident Office:

555 West Beach Street, Suite 302
San Diego, CA 92101
Tel: (619) 293-6184

REGION 22 (New Jersey)

Federal Building, Room 1600
970 Broad Street
Newark, NJ 07102
Tel: (201) 645-2100
William A. Pascarell, Regional Director

REGION 24 (Puerto Rico, U.S. Virgin Islands)

Federal Building, Room 591
150 Avenue Carlos E. Chardon, Room 591
Hato Rey, PR 00918
Tel: (809) 766-5347
Mary Zelma Asseo, Regional Director

REGION 25 (Indiana, Kentucky)

Federal Office Building, Room 238
575 North Pennsylvania Street
Indianapolis, IN 46204
Tel: (317) 226-7430
Roberto G. Chavarry, Regional Director

REGION 26 (Arkansas, Mississippi, Tennessee)

Mid-Memphis Tower Building, Suite 800
1407 Union Avenue
P.O. Box 41559
Memphis, TN 38104
Tel: (901) 544-0018
Gerard P. Fleischat, Regional Director

Resident Offices:

425 W. Capital, Suite 375
Little Rock, AR 72201
Tel: (501) 324-6311

Federal Building
801 Broadway
Nashville, TN 37203
Tel: (615) 736-5922

REGION 27 (Colorado, Idaho, Montana, Nebraska, Wyoming)

600 17th Street
Denver, CO 80202
Tel: (303) 844-3551
B. Allan Benson, Regional Director

REGION 28 (Arizona, New Mexico, Nevada, Texas)

234 North Central Avenue, Suite 440
Phoenix, AZ 85004
Tel: (602) 379-3361
Roy H. Garner, Regional Director

Resident Offices:

505 Marquette Avenue, N.W. Suite 1820
Albuquerque, NM 87102
Tel: (505) 766-3800

U.S. Post Office/Courthouse Building, Room 565
615 E. Houston Street
San Antonio, TX 78205
Tel: (210) 229-6140

600 Las Vegas Blvd., South, Suite 400
Las Vegas, NV 89101
Tel: (702) 388-6416

REGION 29 (New York)

75 Clinton Street, 4th Floor
Brooklyn, N.Y. 11201
Tel: (718) 330-7713
Alvin Blyer, Regional Director

REGION 30 (Michigan, Wisconsin)

310 West Wisconsin Avenue, Suite 700
Milwaukee, WI 53203
Tel: (414) 297-3861
Philip Bloedorn, Regional Director

REGION 31 (California)

Federal Building, Room 12100
11000 Wilshire Boulevard
Los Angeles, CA 90024
Tel: (310) 575-7351
James J. McDermott, Regional Director

REGION 32 (California, Nevada)

1301 Clay Street
Oakland, CA 94612
Tel: (510) 637-3300
James S. Scott, Regional Director

REGION 33 (Illinois, Iowa)

300 Hamilton Boulevard, Suite 200
Peoria, IL 61602
Tel: (309) 671-7080
Glenn A. Zipp, Regional Director

REGION 34 (Connecticut)

One Commercial Plaza
Hartford, CT 06103
Tel: (203) 240-3522
Peter B. Hoffman, Regional Director

HEADQUARTERS

1099 14th Street., N.W.
Washington, D.C. 20570
Tel: (202) 273-1000

BOARD MEMBERS:

William B. Gould IV, Chairman
(term expires August 1998)

Wilma B. Liebman
(term expires December 2002)

Peter T. Hurtgen
(term expires August 2001)

J. Robert Brame
(term expires August 2000)

Sarah M. Fox
(term expires December 1999)

General Counsel: Frederick L. Feinstein
(term expires August 1998)

N L R B   C A S E   O R D E R   F O R M

Please send me copies of the following NLRB decisions. I am enclosing _____ in payment ($5.00 per
decision).

_____

Name

_____

Address

_____

Name of Case   *Volume*   *Page #*

_____ _____ NLRB_____

_____ _____ NLRB_____

_____ _____ NLRB_____

_____ _____ NLRB_____

_____ _____ NLRB_____

_____ _____ NLRB_____

_____ _____ NLRB_____

_____ _____ NLRB_____

Mail to: Work Rights Press
            678 Massachusetts Avenue
            Box 391887
            Cambridge, MA 02139-0008

B O O K   O R D E R   F O R M

Please send me:

_____ copies of *The Legal Rights of Union Stewards* (English edition)

_____ copies of *The Legal Rights of Union Stewards* (Spanish edition)

_____ copies of *The FMLA Handbook: A Practical Guide to the Family and Medical Leave Act for Union Members and Stewards*

All books are $9.95 per copy. Shipping expenses are $2.00 for the first copy and $.50 each for each additional copy, up to a maximum of $7.00.

Total enclosed: $ _____.

_____

Name

_____

Address

_____

Mail to: Work Rights Press
             678 Massachusetts Avenue
             Box 391887
             Cambridge, MA 02139-0008

Bulk rates for orders of 25 or more available upon request.

Telephone: 1-800-576-4552